DIAMOND

THE PHOENIX OF CRYPTO

2013—2014—2015—2016—2017
A CONCISE DIAMOND HISTORY BOOK

Diamond—The Phoenix of Crypto

by Christopher P. Thompson

Copyright © 2017 by Christopher P. Thompson

Book Author by Christopher P. Thompson

Book Design by C. Ellis

ISBN—13: 978-1977849809
ISBN—10: 1977849806

DIAMOND

THE PHOENIX OF CRYPTO

2013—2014—2015—2016—2017
A CONCISE DIAMOND HISTORY BOOK

CHRISTOPHER P. THOMPSON

CONTENTS

Introduction	....	8-9
What is Diamond?	....	10
Why use Diamond?	....	11
Is Diamond Money?	....	12
Coin Specification	....	13
Milestone Timeline	....	14-16
Proof of Stake	....	17
Blockchain	....	18
Block Reward	....	19
DMD Multipool Mining	....	20
DMD Cloudmining	....	21
Cryptocurrency Exchanges	....	22
Community	....	23
A Concise History of Diamond	....	25
1 Launch of the Diamond Blockchain	....	26-31
2 Resurrection of Diamond	....	32-39
3 Diamond Evolution Version Two	....	40-43
4 Diamond First Year Anniversary	....	44-49
5 Proof of Work Block Reward Reduced	....	50-55
6 Diamond Second Year Anniversary	....	56-61
7 Legendary Ten	....	62-67
8 Diamond Third Year Anniversary	....	68-73
9 Market Capitalisation Began to Surge	....	74-83
10 Transition to New DMD V3 Blockchain	....	84-89
Appendix	....	91
News Article One	....	92-93
News Article Two	....	94-95
News Article Three	....	96-97

INTRODUCTION

Since the inception of Bitcoin in 2008, thousands of cryptocurrencies or decentralised blockchains have been launched. Most ventures into the crypto sphere have not gone to plan as their founders would have hoped. Nevertheless, there are currently hundreds of crypto related projects which are succeeding.

This book covers the history of Diamond, an open-source, publicly distributed cryptocurrency. It was launched on the 13th July 2013 as a Scrypt (hashing algorithm) proof of work/stake (timestamping algorithm) blockchain. Since that time, there have been challenges which have been overcome by the development team and members of the community. A team of trusted people (DMD Foundation) are responsible for its wellbeing. Major topics covered in this book include:

- Launch of the Diamond, DMD, blockchain (July 2013)

- Diamond resurrected (November 2013)

- Hashing algorithm changed from Scrypt to Groestl (April 2014)

- Official DMD Multipool went live (July 2014)

- Official DMD Cloudmining went live (September 2014)

- Bittrex initiated the trading pair DMD/BTC on their exchange (May 2015)

- Legendary Ten auctions began (December 2015)

- Legendary Ten auctions ended (February 2016)

- Market Capitalisation surpassed US$1,000,000 for the first time (April 2017)

- Diamond DMD V3 Whitepaper published (July 2017)

- Original blockchain ended and the V3 blockchain began (September 2017)

INTRODUCTION

To be specific, this book covers a concise chronological series of events from the 13th July 2013 to the 14th September 2017. This is over four years of history. During this time, interest in Diamond has attracted growing interest from inside and outside the cryptocurrency space.

You may have bought this book because Diamond, DMD, is your favourite cryptographic blockchain. Alternatively, you may be keen to find out how it all began. I have presented the information henceforth without going into too much technical discussion about Diamond. If you would like to investigate further, I recommend that you read material currently available online at the official website at https://bit.diamonds/

If you choose to purchase a certain amount of DMD, please do not buy more than you can afford to lose.

Enjoy the book :D

WHAT IS DIAMOND?

Diamond is a cryptocurrency or digital decentralised currency used via the Internet. It is described as a payment network without the need for a central authority such as a bank or other central clearing house. It allows the end user to store or transfer value anywhere in the world with the use of a personal computer, laptop or smartphone. Cryptography has been implemented and coded into the network allowing the user to send currency through a decentralised (no centre point of failure), open source (anyone can review the code), peer-to-peer network. Cryptography also controls the creation of staked DMD.

The Diamond network protocol was created by adopting features from Bitcoin, Litecoin, Novacoin, Luckycoin, Florincoin and others. In particular, the random block proof of work characteristic of Luckycoin as incorporated. As was the case with many cryptocurrencies launched in 2013, the code of preceding coins was adopted and a few parameters were changed. After just one month, Diamond was abandoned by its founder/original developers.

Diamond was resurrected in late 2013 by user "zuper". It was again revitalised in April 2014 by a new team consisting of Aleksander Mesor (user "popshot") and Helmut Siedl (user "cryptonit"). These two individuals are respectively the CEO (Chief Executive Officer) and CVO (Chief Visionary Officer) of the DMD Foundation. They have been committed to the Diamond project since April 2014.

On the official Diamond website, the description of the coin is:

> *"Diamond (DMD) is a non-government controlled digital currency that allows people to send money anywhere in the world instantly, securely and at near zero cost. Moreover, DMD Diamond aims to empower people to achieve financial freedom by making every DMD Diamond coin an interest bearing asset with high annual interest rate. This modern age financial instrument makes an excellent storage of value that is supported by the network protocols, infrastructure and services."*

WHY USE DIAMOND?

Like all cryptocurrencies, people have chosen to adopt Diamond as a medium of exchange/storage through personal choice. An innovative feature of the coin, an affinity towards the brand or high confidence in the community could be reasons why they have done so. Key benefits of using Diamond are:

- It is a useful medium of exchange via which value can be transferred internationally for a fraction of the cost of other conventional methods.

- Diamond eliminates the need for a trusted third party such as a bank, clearing house or other centralised authority (e.g. PayPal). All transactions are solely from one person to another (peer-to-peer).

- Diamond has the potential to engage people worldwide who are without a bank account (unbanked).

- Diamond is immune from the effects of hyperinflation, unlike the current fiat monetary systems around the world.

Other reasons officially cited for using Diamond are:

- Scarce —there will be only 4.38 million DMD created
- Valuable —a high interest bearing asset (decreases over time)
- Secure —high security due to advanced cryptography
- Brand —Diamond is a solid name of trust and high reputation
- Fast —confirms transactions quickly (4x faster than BTC)
- Ecological —proof of stake timestamping is environmentally friendly

IS DIAMOND MONEY?

Money is a form of acceptable, convenient and valued medium of payment for goods and services within an economy. It allows two parties to exchange goods or services without the need to barter. This eradicates the potential situation where one party of the two may not want what the other has to offer. The main properties of money are:

- **As a medium of exchange**—money can be used as a means to buy/sell goods/services without the need to barter.

- **A unit of account**—a common measure of value wherever one is in the world.

- **Portable**—easily transferred from one party to another. The medium used can be easily carried.

- **Durable**—all units of the currency can be lost, but not destroyed.

- **Divisible**—each unit can be subdivided into smaller fractions of that unit.

- **Fungible**— each unit of account is the same as every other unit within the medium (1 DMD= 1 DMD).

- **As a store of value**—it sustains its purchasing power (what it can buy) over long periods of time.

Diamond easily satisfies the first six characteristics. Taking into account the last characteristic, the value of Diamond, like all currencies, comes from people willing to accept it as a medium of exchange for payment of goods or services. Additionally, it must be a secure way to store personal wealth. As it gets adopted by more individuals or merchants, its intrinsic value will increase accordingly.

COIN SPECIFICATION

Since the birth of Diamond, its coin specification has changed a few times. At the time of publication of this book, its current specification is:

Coin Symbol:	DMD
Unit of Account:	DMD
Time of Announcement:	13th July 2013 at 23:48:18 UTC
Time of Original Launch:	13th July 2013 at 06:22:11 UTC
Block Number One Generated:	14th September 2017 (V3 Blockchain)
Founder:	User "JohnLuc"
Chief Executive Officer (CEO):	Aleksander Mesor
Chief Visionary Officer (CVO):	Helmut Siedl
Chief Technology Officer (CTO):	Christian Knoepke
Hashing Algorithm:	Groestl
Timestamping Algorithm:	Proof of stake (with masternodes)
Address Begins With:	d
Total Coins:	4,380,000 DMD
Block Time:	135 seconds (PoS)
Reward Halving:	None (block reward decreases gradually)
Pre-mine:	None

MILESTONE TIMELINE

13th July 2013	—Original blockchain launched at 06:22:11 UTC
13th July 2013	—Diamond announced at 23:48:18 UTC
23rd July 2013	—Coins-e initiated the DMD/BTC trading pair
26th July 2013	—Cryptsy initiated the DMD/BTC trading pair
28th July 2013	—Version 1.1 Windows wallet client released
13th August 2013	—Last comment posted by user "JohnLuc"
13th November 2013	—Diamond announced as taken over
1st December 2013	—Version 1.0.1 Windows wallet client released
16th December 2013	—Version 1.0.2 Windows wallet client released
16th December 2013	—Second Diamond Bitcointalk thread created
19th December 2013	—Diamond added to www.coinmarketcap.com
30th December 2013	—First Diamond related comment by user "cryptonit"

2014

7th January 2014	—First Diamond related comment by user "popshot"
11th January 2014	—www.facebook.com/dmdcoin was founded
23rd January 2014	—First tweet posted at @dmdcoin
18th February 2014	—Version 1.0.3 Windows wallet client released
1st March 2014	—Diamond added to www.coinpayments.net
14th March 2014	—Version 1.0.4 Windows wallet client released
22nd April 2014	—Third Diamond Bitcointalk thread created
30th April 2014	—Version 2.0.0 Windows wallet client released
2nd May 2014	—Groestl replaced Scrypt as the hashing algorithm
4th May 2014	—Version 2.0.1 Windows wallet client released
8th May 2014	—Version 2.0.1 Mac OS X wallet client released
9th May 2014	—Sharexcoin initiated the DMD/BTC trading pair
11th May 2014	—Allcrypt initiated the DMD/BTC trading pair

MILESTONE TIMELINE

13th June 2014	—Version 2.0.2.1 wallet clients released
26th June 2014	—Total DMD generated surpassed 450,000
26th June 2014	—Proof of stake became operational at 50% p.a.
17th July 2014	—alcurEx initiated the DMD/BTC trading pair
23rd July 2014	—DMD Multipool went fully live
17th August 2014	—Usecryptos initiated the DMD/BTC trading pair
5th September 2014	—Version 2.0.3.2 wallet clients released
20th September 2014	—Version 2.0.4 wallet clients released
30th September 2014	—DMD Cloudmining became operational

2015

13th January 2015	—Comkort initiated four DMD related trading pairs
28th January 2015	—DMD Reactor project was born
18th February 2015	—Over 100,000 payed out of DMD Multipool
8th April 2015	—Version 2.0.5.5 wallet clients released
12th April 2015	—Total DMD generated surpassed 1,000,000
1st May 2015	—Bittrex initiated live trading of DMD against BTC
3rd June 2015	—Cryptopia initiated seven DMD related trading pairs
10th July 2015	—DMD Clouding redistributed over 100,000 DMD
12th July 2015	—ATH 2015 market capitalisation at US$687,636
13th July 2015	—2nd Anniversary Cake Competition won by user "hallared" who was rewarded 250 DMD
10th December 2015	—Legendary Ten auctions began

2016

19th January 2016	—Total DMD generated surpassed 1,500,000
19th January 2016	—Proof of stake reduced from 50% p.a. to 25% p.a.

MILESTONE TIMELINE

9th February 2016	—Last two Legendary Ten Diamonds sold
10th May 2016	—Version 2.1.0.1 Windows wallet client released
13th May 2016	—Version 2.1.0.1 Mac OS X wallet client released
8th June 2016	—Version 2.1.0.3 Windows wallet client released
11th June 2016	—Version 2.1.0.3 Mac OS X wallet client released
8th July 2016	—Version 2.1.0.4 wallet clients released
13th July 2016	—3rd Anniversary Cake Competition won by user "hallared" who was rewarded 233 DMD
17th August 2016	—Promotional video for DMD uploaded to YouTube titled "bit.diamonds	WHAT IS YOUR CHOICE?"

2017

15th January 2017	—DMD Multipool and Cloudmining combined had redistributed over 300,000 DMD
3rd April 2017	—Market capitalisation surpassed US$1,000,000 for the first time ever
24th April 2017	—New flat version of the DMD logo unveiled
19th May 2017	—One DMD unit of account priced above US$1 for the first time since 23rd January 2014
28th June 2017	—All time high DMD market capitalisation (before V3 Blockchain went live) attained at US$19,106,393.
13th July 2017	—For the third time running, user "hallared" won the year's cake anniversary competition
13th July 2017	—DMD V3 Whitepaper published
29th August 2017	—DMD Wallet 2.0 to 3.0 transition guide published
13th September 2017	—Last block of V2 Blockchain timestamped
14th September 2017	—First block of V3 Blockchain timestamped

PROOF OF STAKE

Proof of stake was independently discovered by Sunny King after he studied the work of Satoshi Nakamoto. It is basically a timestamping algorithm which helps to secure the network in order to sustain decentralisation and validate transactions. Therefore, no third party needs to be trusted to verify and add transactions to the blockchain. It was introduced into Peercoin, PPC, alongside proof of work on the 19th August 2012. It has been adopted, and sometimes improved upon, by many other cryptocurrencies over the years.

Diamond was originally launched as a hybrid proof of work/stake cryptocurrency. It was not until the 26th June 2014 that the proof of stake part of the algorithm (operated independently of proof of work) became operational at 50% p.a. This reduced to 25% p.a. on the 19th January 2016. On the 14th September 2017, the Diamond network began using just proof of stake. Only wallet clients which stay connected to the network are permitted to claim network stake rewards (a certain portion of 35% of the block reward). The other 65% of block rewards are available to masternode holders. A masternode is defined as:

"Diamond Masternodes are computers that are constantly connected to the Diamond Network and perform certain tasks allowing DMD Diamond to achieve faster and more private transactions. To run a Diamond Masternode one is required to have 10,000 DMD in their balance, as collateral, and fulfil other requirements imposed by the protocol. For their dedicated service, Diamond Masternodes are rewarded with 65% of network rewards. Diamond Masternodes form a backbone that is a part of a technological mix which powers services and apps of a wider DMD Diamond ecosystem."

The DMD Foundation are confident that masternodes will allow further development which looked impossible beforehand. Five masternodes are owned by the foundation, but these 50,000 DMD cannot be moved or spent (ghostcoins).

BLOCKCHAIN

Every cryptocurrency has a corresponding blockchain within its decentralised network protocol. Diamond is no different in this sense. A blockchain is simply described as a general public ledger of all transactions and blocks ever executed since the very first block. In addition, it continuously updates in real time each time a new block is successfully mined. Blocks enter the blockchain in such a manner that each block contains the hash of the previous one. It is therefore utterly resistant to modification along the chain since each block is related to the prior one. Consequently, the problem of doubling-spending is solved.

Two blockchains have served the Diamond project. Originally, the first blockchain launched on the 13th July 2013. A new blockchain launched on the 14th September 2017 (rewritten protocol parameters).

As a means for members of the general public to view the blockchain, web developers have designed and implemented block explorers. They tend to present different layouts, statistics and charts. Some explorers are more extensive in terms of the information given. Usual statistics included are:

- **Height of block** —the block number of the network.

- **Time of block** —the time at which the block was timestamped to the blockchain.

- **Transactions** —the number of transactions in that particular block.

- **Total Sent** —the total amount of cryptocurrency sent in that particular block.

- **Block Reward** —how many coins were generated in the block (added to the overall coin circulation).

BLOCK REWARD

A reward is successfully transferred to the miner/minter each time a block is timestamped. Block rewards have been decreasing over time as a way to reduce the inflation and make it more difficult to acquire DMD units of account.

Initially, only miners were able to compete for an average 1,500 DMD generated daily. Most blocks successfully timestamped had an associated reward of 1 DMD and a few lucky miners took advantage of 2, 8, 30 DMD blocks. This ended on the 2nd May 2014 when the block reward became a static 1.05 DMD.

On the 26th June 2014, proof of stake became operational at 50% p.a. Wallet client users, or users of the DMD Multipool or Cloudmining services, could now obtain DMD units of account without mining them directly.

On the 12th April 2015, as soon as the 1,000,000th DMD unit of account had been generated at 09:07:22 UTC, the proof of work block reward reduced by 80% to 0.21 DMD. Instead of one PoW/PoS block taking, on average, 60/600 seconds to be timestamped, they both changed to an average of 100 seconds.

On the 19th January 2016, the proof of stake reward reduced to 25% p.a. It had become more difficult for people to acquire DMD via staking.

At the present time, Diamond cannot be mined directly via proof of work. It can only be obtained by proof of stake. Those who stake compete for a percentage of a certain block reward (135 seconds block time). Overall, stakers acquire 35% of the total network block rewards, whereas masternode holders get the remaining 65%

Over the longer term, the rate at which DMD unit of accounts get added to the overall money supply will decrease. The DMD Foundation will strive to introduce additional methods in order to keep the supply below the 4.38 million coin cap. Ultimately, this will create conditions that lead to deflation.

DMD MULTIPOOL MINING

Multipool mining is a method by which users can acquire cryptocurrencies without directly mining them. DMD Multipool miners are able to mine other profitable coins via a myriad of other hashing algorithms such as SHA256, Scrypt, Keccak, X11, X13 and so on. They are rewarded a certain amount of DMD, which are bought straight from the open market, depending on the hashing power they commit. This has had the advantage of creating buy pressure, so has helped increase the value of Diamond. It went live on the 23rd July 2014 at https://multipool.bit.diamonds/

On the 18th February 2015, the total accumulated number of DMD payed out of the DMD Multipool exceeded 100,000. This accounted for over 10% of all DMD generated at that time.

It is currently the only way for miners to acquire DMD. Miners were able to mine DMD directly, but this became impossible on the 14th September 2017. In September 2017, the following is displayed on the official DMD Multipool website:

"Mining on the pool is through NiceHash. We add zero on top of
their standard 2% fees. Any BTC (including Nicehash Payouts) send to your
DMD Multipool BTC address is converted to DMD send to your DMD address."

DMD CLOUDMINING

DMD Cloudmining was introduced to the community in September 2014. Pay outs to shareholders commenced on the 30th September 2014. Many people who have participated in the service have been very happy with their returns. Still active today, it helps keep the Diamond network more secure by actively staking DMD units of account which otherwise would have been idle on, for example, cryptocurrency exchanges.

On the official Diamond website at https://bit.diamonds/, the following description of the DMD Cloudmining service is displayed:

"Diamond Cloud Mining is a network support scheme where supporters are granted regular, hassle free, forever flowing stream of Diamonds. It's easy, it's profitable and makes power bills a thing of the past.

We offer our 0% commission service to people who wouldn't necessarily want to waste their time and energy on spending a few hours a day to stay up to date with Cloud Mining market to get favourable deals on attractive terms, and follow a clear earnings conserving path of reinvestments so the potential is not wasted. At the same time we handle all support donations with uttermost care."

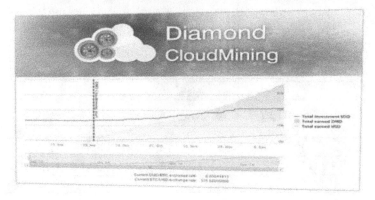

CRYPTOCURRENCY EXCHANGES

A cryptocurrency exchange is a site on which registered users can buy or sell Diamond against Bitcoin, BTC. Some exchanges require users to fully register by submitting certain documentation including proof of identity and address. On the other hand, most exchanges only require users to register with a simple username and password with the use of a currently held e-mail address.

As well as being the method by which people can buy or sell DMD, exchanges serve the purpose of setting the value of the coin. One unit of DMD account reached a high of US$8.84 on the 28th June 2017, but has since ascended above US12 after the launch of DMD V3.

Coins-e was the first exchange to initiate live trading of Diamond on the 23rd July 2013. Diamond is no longer active on this exchange. Other exchanges have also added Diamond to their platforms, but only Bittrex remains active. It is evident in the history pages of this book that both the market capitalisation (the value of all DMD units of account generated) and US$ per 1 DMD have shown growth/decline. Below is a list of all exchanges which initiated DMD/BTC trading:

DATE DMD TRADING INITIATED	EXCHANGE	DIAMOND TRADING STATUS
23rd July 2013	Coins-e	CLOSED
26th July 2013	Cryptsy	CLOSED
9th May 2014	Sharexcoin	CLOSED
11th May 2014	Allcrypt	CLOSED
17th July 2014	alcurEx	CLOSED
17th August 2014	Usecryptos	CLOSED
13th January 2015	Comkort	CLOSED
1st May 2015	Bittrex	ACTIVE
3rd June 2015	Cryptopia	CLOSED

COMMUNITY

A community is a social unit or network that shares common values and goals. It derives from the old French word "comuntee". This, in turn, originates from "communitas" in Latin (communis; things held in common). Diamond has a community consisting of an innumerable number of people who have the coin's wellbeing and future goal at heart. The majority of these people prefer fictitious names with optional avatars. DMD Foundation members are primarily responsible and devoted to the project. Three individuals part of this foundation are:

- Aleksander Mesor (user "popshot") —Chief Executive Officer (CEO)
- Helmut Siedl (user "cryptonit") —Chief Visionary Officer (CVO)
- Christian Knoepke (user "Limx Dev") —Chief Technology Officer (CTO)

Users "crazyivan", "shveicar" and "metamorphin" are also part of the foundation.

At the time of publication, there are social media sites (and other official websites) on which discussion and development of Diamond take place. These are:

- https://bit.diamonds/ Official Diamond Website
- https://twitter.com/dmdcoin/ Official Diamond Twitter Account
- https://www.facebook.com/dmdcoin/ Official Diamond Facebook Page
- https://bitcointalk.org/index.php?topic=580725.0/

In essence, the community surrounding and participating in the development of Diamond is the backbone of the coin. Without a following, the prospects of future adoption and utilisation are starkly limited. Diamond belongs to all those who use it, not just to the developers who aid its progression.

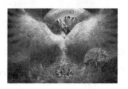

A CONCISE HISTORY OF DIAMOND

LIST OF CHAPTERS

1   —LAUNCH OF THE DIAMOND BLOCKCHAIN
2   —RESURRECTION OF DIAMOND
3   —DIAMOND EVOLUTION VERSION TWO
4   —DIAMOND FIRST YEAR ANNIVERSARY
5   —PROOF OF WORK BLOCK REWARD REDUCED
6   —DIAMOND SECOND YEAR ANNIVERSARY
7   —LEGENDARY TEN
8   —DIAMOND THIRD YEAR ANNIVERSARY
9   —MARKET CAPITALISATION BEGAN TO SURGE
10   —TRANSITION TO NEW DMD V3 BLOCKCHAIN

I.   BLOCKCHAIN LAUNCHED ON THE 13TH JULY 2013

II.   AN EXCHANGE CALLED COINS-E INITIATED DMD TRADING

III.   AN EXCHANGE CALLED CRYPTSY INITIATED DMD TRADING

IV.   FOUNDER LAST COMMENTED ON THE 13TH AUGUST 2013

V.   DIAMOND DEVELOPMENT BECAME LACKLUSTRE

1

LAUNCH OF THE DIAMOND BLOCKCHAIN

"Diamond combines the best from Bitcoin/Litecoin/Novacoin/Luckycoin/Florincoin, it uses both Proof of Work and Proof of Stake. This provides a excellent resistance to 51% attack. It also combines the random block feature from Luckycoin, making it the first coin in Pow/PoS category to use random blocks." - user "JohnLuc"

Similar to how almost all other cryptocurrencies are announced, Diamond became known to the wider Bitcoin community via an online forum called Bitcointalk. A user fictitiously known as "JohnLuc" (the founder/original developer) created the first official Diamond thread on Bitcointalk titled "[ANN] Diamond DMD - new PoW/PoS coin | Super random blocks | Only 4.38 mil total" at 23:48:18 UTC on the 13th July 2013.

Before the creation of the above thread, blocks had already been mined and timestamped to the blockchain. To be specific, 1,053 blocks had generated a total of 1,103 DMD. It was therefore the case that the public launch began as soon as miners, except for the developers, had knowhow of how to mine DMD. As is evident in the quote above, the founder adopted features from previously launched cryptocurrencies including Bitcoin, Litecoin and Luckycoin.

Block number one timestamped to the Diamond blockchain at 06:22:11 UTC on the 13th July 2013. A single DMD unit of account was generated as can be seen below. Also, during its Scrypt proof of work mining phase, Diamond was mined at a linear rate (average) of 1,500 DMD per day including bonus blocks. Everyday there were:

Block Description	Reward per Block	Number of Blocks	Total DMD
Regular	1	1,426	1,426
Bonus	2	10	20
Super	8	3	24
Super+	30	1	30
Total		1,440	1,500

What follows are the first mined bonus, super and super+ blocks on the blockchain:

Block #1 (Reward 1 DMD) July 13th 2013 at 06:22:11 AM UTC

Block #30 (Reward 30 DMD) July 13th 2013 at 06:32:50 AM UTC

Block #144 (Reward 2 DMD) July 13th 2013 at 08:28:12 AM UTC

Block #209 (Reward 8 DMD) July 13th 2013 at 09:35:42 AM UTC

One day after the launch, user "JohnLuc" uploaded a minor update to the Windows client (no Mac client existed at this time) so that the hashrate (total processing power directed to the network by miners) correctly displayed. This was not a mandatory update. Download links and sources were accordingly updated.

On the 21st July, there were some users on Bitcointalk who thought the founder was not being active enough in supporting the coin. A roadmap was suggested to help aid the project forward. On the other hand, there were those who called for patience and calm.

On the 23rd July 2013 at 17:05:50 UTC, user "minus" announced Coins-e as the first cryptocurrency exchange to initiate trading of Diamond:

"Diamond is now listed now on Coins-E

https://www.coins-e.com/exchange/DMD_BTC/

Cheers"

However, trading ceased immediately after its introduction due to the platform's inability to properly process deposits. They relaunched the DMD/BTC trading pair two days later. Prior to Coins-e, users had been trading DMD with each other on the DMD Bitcointalk forum thread in exchange for BTC, LTC, PPC and so on.

It was not long before live trading of Diamond commenced on a second exchange. Cryptsy did just that on the 26th July 2013. User "BitJohn" welcomed fans of DMD to the www.cryptsy.com family. Some supporters of Diamond had been tirelessly and relentlessly contacting Cryptsy via message to get it listed there. User "JohnLuc" described this event as wonderful. Other users were also very enthused about the news. It was an exchange based in Delray Beach, Florida, USA and began operations on the 20th May 2013. It closed its doors in January 2016 due to dubious activities.

On the 28th July at 18:03:41 UTC, user "JohnLuc" notified the community that version 1.1 of the wallet client had been released. It introduced new checkpoints for higher security. It was not mandatory, but recommended as a way to make the network more secure.

Towards the end of the month, user "JohnLuc" understandably regarded Diamond, DMD, as undervalued. He saw immense potential ahead similar to other successful cryptocurrencies in the space. One defining feature of Diamond, he pointed out, was the 4.38 million total cap (roughly five times less than Bitcoin's total coin cap).

Concerns were growing as to whether the founder of Diamond was being purposefully low key or had totally abandoned the coin. On the 3rd August, user "Pmalek" requested greater participation from the founder. Three days later, he again wanted to know what plans user "JohnLuc" had to take Diamond forward.

On the 10th August at 22:19:07 UTC, after much thought and deliberation, user "Pmalek" decided to create a Bitcointalk thread titled "[PROPOSAL] Let there be DMD Takeover!" on which he described his devotion to see Diamond shine:

"I am starting this topic because I like this coin! It has great name, nice specs, and real bad support. It would be a shame for this coin to die…"

The penultimate recorded comment from user "JohnLuc" on the official Diamond Bitcointalk thread was posted on the 13th August at 12:02:23 UTC. He said:

"I don't see where come up this takeover idea. I made the coin - the first pow/pos with random blocks, and I maintained it until it hits cryptsy, it's a great success.. I will continue maintain it if there are any issues - so far the only minor issue is the pos payout, which given small dmd payout, is a normal thing.

I did all the work without premine, and the results seem that people are just never satisfied. I am really a developer, not a promotor, so if you think the coin is not promo'd enough, please do it, it is a work of the community, not the developer.

Guys, this is a public source project, if you guys are not happy, make any changes yourself, as long as the community accept them. Don't do the stupid things like start another blockchain etc. Because if you know how to do it, then you better start another coin. And don't just talk, talk is too easy and cheap, only talking is not worth anything. Again the code is there, you are welcome to make any changes (and take over) there."

A few minutes later, he posted his last comment in relation to Diamond. He had no problem with anyone else taking over the project. He made reference to the fact that it had always been a "public source project". He encouraged the community to enhance it as long as the community agreed on the way forward.

During the days which followed, efforts were being made to search for people who could fill the vacancy left by the founder. There was a strong feeling that he had definitely abandoned Diamond. Some initiatives put forward to help keep the coin active included:

- A bounty was commissioned (100 DMD) for someone to create a block explorer. User "HippieTech" was adamant that the lack of an explorer had been a major factor holding the coin back.

- There were calls for DMD to be removed temporarily from both Coins-e and Cryptsy so as to reduce the dumping/selling of the coin by miners.

Over the next several months, there were hardly any updates or enthusiasm from the waning Diamond community. There were still sporadically posted comments and responses on the official Diamond Bitcointalk thread, but nothing substantial happened. Some members of the community saw great potential, but were disappointed. A few promised to keep mining the coin.

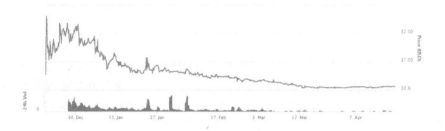

I.   USER "ZUPER" TOOK CONTROL OVER DEVELOPMENT

II.   2ND DMD BITCOINTALK THREAD CREATED ON THE 16TH DEC 2013

III.   WWW.COINMARKETCAP.COM ADDED DMD ON THE 19TH DEC 2013

IV.   COINPAYMENTS.NET INTEGRATED DMD ON THE 1ST MARCH 2014

V.   MARKET CAPITALSATION HAD GRADUALLY DECREASED

2

RESURRECTION OF DIAMOND

"We are thrilled to announce that the DMD community is back!
We have taken control of the future of this amazing crypto currency by taking
over its development and maintenance." —user "zuper"

When all hope seemed to have been lost, an individual or group known as user "zuper", on the 13th November 2013, announced their commitment towards making Diamond a success. They described themselves as a team from Greece.

On the 24th November 2013 at 02:18:16 UTC, user "zuper" was quoted as saying:

"Hello all! We are looking for developers in order to update the diamond client.
Please let us know if anyone are interested in joining to our community."

In addition to the above, user "zuper" asked if anyone wanted to compile the source code. Two days later, an update to the code was available at https://github.com/DiamondCrypto/diamondcoin/. Work was well underway to rescue Diamond from the sheer lack of development during the last three months.

On the first day of December 2013, a brand new Windows wallet client (version 1.0.1) was released. User "zuper" had fixed an "invalid wallet download link". It was accessible from their own mining pool at http://www.dmdpool.net. One user in particular, "Sheinsha", was happy to see the revival of the Diamond community:

"COMMUNITY IS BACK ACTIVE AGAIN + PRICE REBOUNDING!!!"

Despite the release of the new wallet client, there were still many issues to solve technically and cosmetically. People requested a new official website and a brand new official Diamond Bitcointalk thread (to solidify the message that a takeover had occurred). Members of the growing community were happy that efforts were being made, but did not deny that confusion existed. A google group had also been created as a way for developers to discuss the next steps at:

http://groups.google.com/forum/#!forum/dmd-community

On the 9th December, there were emerging signs that a 51% attack on the DMD network protocol had occurred. On that day at 21:00:25 UTC, user "zuper" reported that the only two active mining pools were inaccessible. As a response, he insisted a hard fork should be implemented and any help was welcome. Cryptsy suspended DMD/BTC trading on their exchange platform indefinitely.

On the 10th December, calls were made for decent developers to take over the project. These calls were a result of impatience by some, and lack of confidence from others, that the coin had little chance of moving forward. This was in spite of user "zuper" saying there was already a plan to release a new client. Another opinion at the time was "For now we should concentrate on fixing the network." There were other users who wanted the coin to "die" or they encouraged those wanting it to survive to just give up. There were constant reports of:

"My new wallet cannot sync: Checkpoint is too old, wait
for blockchain to download or notify developers."

On the 13th December at 07:07:51 UTC, a long awaited Diamond block explorer finally went live. User "Tripmode" posted the following:

"I have set up a Diamond Block Explorer http://www.diamondblocks.info
It is using open source software called Abe."

The new development team were happy to witness the sustained recovery.

On the 16th December, user "Palmdetroit" posted details of an updated Windows wallet client (version 1.0.2). Also on this day at 09:01:54 UTC, a new official Diamond Bitcointalk thread titled "[ANN] Diamond (DMD) Takeover! Update v1.0.2 | NEW website, pool, block-explorer" was created. The opening post was:

"We are thrilled to announce that the DMD community is back!
We have taken control of the future of this amazing crypto currency by taking over its development and maintenance!

Coin settings have been left intact:
- Only 4.38 million DMD to be created in eight years. A little bit more than 200,000 coins have been created since the original open launch in July 2013, so it's still open to very early adopters!
- The production curve is linear: 1,500 coins are created each day in 1,440 blocks (one block every minute). No block reward halving ever.
- No pre-mining, insta-mining or other shenanigan! This is a 100% fair coin.
- Each block contains 1 DMD. Every day,
ten random blocks (called bonus blocks) contain 2 DMDs,
three random blocks (called super blocks) contain 8 DMDs,
and one random block (called a super+ block) contains 30 DMDs.
- Difficulty retargeting at every block.

Get on board and help us spread the word on this amazing currency!

More info coming up soon..."

A new official Diamond Bitcointalk thread signalled a re-birth of the project. It followed on from news that both recognised DMD mining pools, dmdpool.net and dmd.minar.cc, had become active again as well as the resumption of trading at Cryptsy after six days of suspension. Unfortunately, the original thread could not be locked because the new team were not in control of it.

On the 19th December 2013, there was positive news which increased the status of Diamond amongst all other cryptocurrencies. Diamond was added to a website on which hundreds of cryptocurrencies can be discovered and then, willingly or not, investigated via displayed links. It is called www.coinmarketcap.com. On this day at 13:22:16 UTC, user "gmg" stated the first estimate of Diamond's market capitalisation at US$132,000. It surpassed US$500,000 later that day. Historical data derived from this website is as follows:

	Low US$	Open US$	Close US$	High US$
19th December	0.554937	0.573386	2.12	2.76
20th December	0.693511	2.22	1.37	1.74
21st December	1.09	1.36	1.29	1.74

As Christmas 2013 drew near, there were understandably few and far between updates or coin related news.

On the 30th December at 17:36:43 UTC, user "cryptonit" posted his first comment on the official Diamond Bitcointalk thread. He was quoted as saying:

"is there any page that give insight into the POS miracle
how to setup and earn dmd with POS. if im sitting on example 1000 dmd
how much POS dmd i can expect for have wallet running 24/7"

The last block timestamped to the blockchain in 2013 was successfully mined via proof of work. A total of 200,442.37036401 DMD had been mined so far.

Block #224,304 (Reward 1 DMD) December 31st 2013 at 11:59:50 PM UTC

Discussion at the end of December 2013 was primarily about how the community could best promote Diamond to a wider audience. One suggestion put forward was to pay an outside professional body to record a promotional video. Other ideas included a more professional official website, guides about proof of stake and a YouTube channel. Plans were afoot to build upon prior successes.

On the 7th January 2014 at 16:52:50 UTC, user "popshot" posted his first comment on the second official Diamond Bitcointalk thread. He was quoted as saying:

"So how many Diamonds there are to be mined? 4.3 million or 210k? There seem to be contradicting information on that.

Is there any sound Marketing strategy in the making? I just hope you are not deluding yourselves about Wall Street investment.

When can we expect a dedicated forum to be up and running along with the website? Is there any time frame /deadline you're working towards?

As much as I like the concept and name of the coin without proper development it's doomed (no matter what you say or wish for)."

After receiving numerous private messages asking him to reveal the next steps of DMD development, user "zuper" posted a short list of his team's basic plan. He politely asked the community if anyone could help with the following:

- To compile a Mac OS X wallet client

- To initiate social media presence

- To create a promotional video

- To contact further cryptocurrency exchanges

He was also happy that the community had become more active. Diamond development now focused on a stable network, functional wallet clients and active trading platforms (Cryptsy being the only one at the time).

Resurrection of Diamond

On the 27th January 2014 at 22:08:38 UTC, user "zuper" announced:

"Hello everyone!
As we promised, new dedicated forum is up and running!

I don't like big words, so everyone interested in Diamond please join 😄
http://www.dmdcoin.net/forum"

This forum is no longer operational. Instead, a new official Diamond forum exists at https://bit.diamonds/community/.

Since the 10th December 2013, Coins-e had not reactivated the DMD/BTC trading pair on their platform. There was a subsequent search for another exchange. CoinEx and Allcrypt were being investigated as possible options.

On the 18th February, a lengthy announcement was posted by user "popshot". He praised the community for enduring the difficult period during which time there were hardly any updates and lack of progress. He understood the lingering doubt about the future of the project. He emphasised the fact that the current developers had other personal commitments which were hindering them from fully devoting their time to Diamond. Users "zuper" and "palmdetroit" were responsible for development at this time.

A few hours later on the 18th February, user "zuper" announced the release of version 1.0.3 of the wallet client. It was necessary to address the low connectivity issues (nodes serving the network). This had to be resolved before proof of stake could work as planned.

On the first day of March 2014, user "popshot" announced that Diamond had been added to www.coinpayments.net. It is an integrated payment gateway service for over 373,000 businesses across 182 different countries. They support over 75 cryptocurrencies. The director of ShibeMint.com submitted the following:

"I have to tip my hat to the people at CoinPayments.net. They've released a stable, robust service to accept cryptocurrency for your online business. I couldn't be happier with the success of the business, and I couldn't have done it without CoinPayments.net"

On the 14th March, version 1.0.4 of the Windows wallet client was made available for installation. It enabled proof of stake at a future day. It was mandatory for users who wanted to stake. Two days later, proof of stake was still not active because too few users had updated.

On the 21st April at 22:17:08 UTC, user "popshot" addressed the community about his intention to make an announcement within the next twenty four hours. In his own words, he finished by saying:

"Everything will be revealed in a new thread. We are no longer a 'takeover' thread but making new fresh steps with our beloved evolved coin."

Over the past few months, the fiat US$ value of one unit of DMD account, and the corresponding daily average market capitalisation, had gradually decreased:

Date	Low US$	Open US$	Close US$	High US$	Market Cap US$
19th December 2013	0.554937	0.573386	2.12	2.76	515,127
19th January 2014	0.555811	0.755694	0.640347	0.759446	170,646
19th February 2014	0.473777	0.488244	0.477883	0.508297	131,963
19th March 2014	0.123561	0.125437	0.123716	0.127068	38,934
19th April 2014	0.136933	0.139563	0.145268	0.145965	49,493

Other events which occurred during this period were:

- On the 1st January, http://diamondblocks.info changed to a new layout thanks to Zaak. The 1996 style design was removed.

- On the 6th January, user "captchunk" created www.reddit.com/r/dmd/. He asked if anyone wanted to become its moderator.

- On the 11th January, www.facebook.com/dmdcoin was founded.

- On the 23rd January, the first tweet was posted on the new Twitter account at @dmdcoin. User "networkcoinage" created it and was willing to turn over the reigns to the developers.

I.   3RD DMD BITCOINTALK THREAD CREATED ON THE 22ND APRIL 2014

II.   HASHING ALGORITHM CHANGED FROM SCRYPT TO GROESTL

III.   SHAREXCOIN AND ALLCRYPT INTEGRATED DMD TRADING

IV.   VERSION 2.0.2.1 CLIENT WAS RELEASED ON THE 13TH JUNE 2014

V.   PoS BECAME OPERATIONAL AT 50% P.A. ON THE 26TH JUNE 2014

3

DIAMOND EVOLUTION
VERSION TWO

"Not everything that seems good at the beginning is good in the long run. We had to evolve in order to reflect the needs of the contemporary market. With the old specification the coin would stop working just after several years while with the improved mechanics it will last at least several decades."—user *"popshot"*

On the 22nd April at 22:06:06 UTC, user "popshot" created the third official Diamond Bitcointalk thread titled "[ANN] Diamond Coin (DMD) Evolution v 2.0 | NEW wallet, coin mechanics, 50% POS". A change of hashing algorithm from Scrypt to Groestl was being tested for implementation into the next update. In addition, a static reward per proof of work block of 1.05 DMD (no more random blocks) would come into effect. One DMD for the miner and 0.05 DMD for the new foundation.

The market capitalisation had increased by ~400% over the last three days:

Date	Low US$	Open US$	Close US$	High US$	Volume (DMD)	Market Cap US$
20th April	0.142785	0.145322	0.183251	0.183963	1,713	51,739
21st April	0.183093	0.183093	0.449185	0.450339	7,438	65,450
22nd April	0.246401	0.750614	0.395263	0.752957	12,912	269,371

On the 30th April 2014, immediately after the network protocol had gone down, the developers decided to proceed with the hard fork to version two. Version two software was then subsequently released. Unfortunately, the code did not function as expected. Further testing was required. The development team had been too ambitious and had, as a consequence, included too much new material.

Two days later, the hard fork kicked in at block number 386,227. Groestl replaced Scrypt as the hashing algorithm of the Diamond network protocol:

Block #386,226 (Reward 1 DMD) May 2nd 2014 at 08:42:33 AM UTC

Block #386,227 (Reward 1.05 DMD) May 2nd 2014 at 08:42:54 AM UTC

On the 4th May, version 2.0.1 of the Windows wallet client was released. The network was described as stable and DMD units of account were being properly transacted between wallet addresses. There were requests from the community to create a mining pool which would support mining via Groestl. Miners were limited to solo mining for the time being.

On the 8th May, user "pcmerc" released version 2.0.1 of the Mac OS X wallet client.

Two exchanges made it possible for their users to buy and sell Diamond. These were:

- Sharexcoin initiated live trading between Bitcoin and Diamond on the 9th May at https://sharexcoin.com/market/DMD_BTC.

- Allcrypt initiated live trading between Bitcoin and Diamond on the 11th May. As of today, this exchange is no longer operational.

On the 31st May at 16:21:51 UTC, user "popshot" said:

"Yes it is coming, as was mentioned before we are in the debugging mode. We are testing all the scenarios and whenever crash happens we find the root cause and fix it."

In relation to the next wallet update, two key dates were as follows:

- On the 5th June, user "vagnavs" advertised for external testers for phase two of beta testing.

- On the 8th June, phase one testing (beta internal) of the next client was complete. Phase two commenced.

On the 13th June, version 2.0.2.1 of the wallet client was released. The switch that would turn on proof of stake was set at 450,000 total coins. On the same day, user "popshot" said:

"A joyous moment has finally arrived. We are delighted and proud to announce new Diamond client with all the fixes we've been working hard to implement. For the first time in Diamond's existence a properly working Proof of Stake functionality is finally here."

On the 26th June, block number 462,905 marked the milestone at which the number of DMD units of account generated to date surpassed 450,000. Proof of stake successfully became operational at 50% per annum. User "popshot" was glad the wait was over. As things stood at the time, difficulty would adjust accordingly to find a PoW and PoS block at 60s and 600s respectively. Both timestamping algorithms were working independent of each other.

> Block #462,904 (Reward 1.05 DMD) June 26th 2014 at 11:01:34 AM UTC

> Block #462,905 (Reward 1.05 DMD) June 26th 2014 at 11:02:45 AM UTC

On the 4th July, user "popshot" posted an update in which he said activation of proof of stake was not the end of the road.

I.   FIRST YEAR ANNIVERSARY CELEBRATED ON THE 13TH JULY 2014

II.   DIAMOND MULTIPOOL WENT FULLY LIVE ON THE 23RD JULY 2014

III.   ALCUREX AND USECRYPTOS INITIATED DMD TRADING

IV.   PROOF OF WORK CEASED, BUT WAS REACTIVATED

V.   DIAMOND CLOUDMINING BEGAN IN SEPTEMBER 2014

4

DIAMOND FIRST YEAR ANNIVERSARY

"It has become our journey, our vector in life, our dream that we have tirelessly pursued sacrificing more than some would be willing to sacrifice." - user "popshot"

Diamond Foundation CEO, user "popshot", was proud to broadcast the celebrations attaining to the first year birthday of the coin. Six developers were stated as being involved with it since the beginning. He admitted that there had been setbacks and loss in faith over the year, but was resolute that the future would bring even better results. He also submitted the following comment:

"If we are fit enough to survive for so long, we are well fit to overcome anything that the future brings; and the thing with the future is that we do not try to predict it, we simply create it."

The last block timestamped to the blockchain during first year was 486,248:

Block #486,248 (Reward 1.05 DMD) July 13th 2014 at 06:21:55 AM UTC

On the 17th July 2014, direct trading between Diamond, DMD, and Bitcoin, BTC, was initiated on the exchange called alcurEx at:

https://alcurex.org/index.php/crypto/market?pair=DMD_BTC/

It is described as a cryptocurrency financing company based in Finland. There were initial problems with depositing/withdrawing Diamond, but the administrators there were quick to resolve this. They consider security as high priority. Diamond is no longer active on alcurEx.

Also on the 17th July, a Diamond related news article was published by an independent cryptocurrency website called CryptoNews247. It was given the title "Diamond 2.0—The Phoenix of Cryptocurrency". It can be read in the appendix of this book on pages 92 and 93.

On the 22nd July, the first automated DMD pay out from the beta DMD Multipool happened. On the following day, after stability tests, user "cryptonit" was proud to announce the full functionality of http://multipool.bit.diamonds/. A method to earn DMD units of account (one possible entry point to acquire DMD) via a selection of other hashing algorithms, instead of Groestl, had become available. A definition of a multipool from www.cryptocompare.com is:

"Multipool mining is the process of jumping across from crypto to crypto currency and mining the most profitable crypto coin at that moment in time. Multi-pool miners will take into account a crypto currencies network mining power and their exchange rates."

Also on the 23rd July, block number 500,000 timestamped to the blockchain. A total of 504,044.52450901 DMD had been mined/minted so far:

Block #500,000 (Reward 1.05 DMD) July 23rd 2014 at 03:36:28 AM UTC

It was clear that people were getting restless about the frequent maintenance periods of the Diamond wallet on Cryptsy. A search to integrate the coin on another major exchange had been on the agenda throughout the summer. One exchange in particular, called Mintpal, was being investigated and contacted. Usecryptos was another possible option. On the 17th August 2014, Diamond won the latest round of voting on Usecryptos and was integrated on that platform as two trading pairs, DMD/USD and DMD/BTC, went live. It was founded in February 2014 in Brazil and moved to Portugal in November that same year.

On the 4th September at 21:03:52 UTC, user "kussaka" won a competition to design graphics for the opening post of the official Diamond Bitcointalk thread. He was rewarded 200 DMD for his work. User "hallared" received 20 DMD for his entry. User "kussaka" initially published his design on the 23rd August at 22:03:22 UTC. As can be seen below, user "popshot" described the colour combination, white as a backdrop to the logo, as beautiful.

On the 5th September 2014, user "danbi" released the relevant updates for version 2.0.3.2 on Github at https://github.com/DMDcoin/Diamond. Later that day, user "popshot" posted download links to the Windows and Mac OS X wallet clients.

Eleven days later, proof of work mining suddenly ceased. It was initially unknown whether the network had been attacked by an external entity or if it was due to an internal fault with the code. After some analysis, reports by user "cryptonit" assured the community the network was still operational. Proof of stake alone was securing the network, but at a slower rate of transactions (average 600 seconds per block found). A vulnerability fixed for proof of stake was not fixed for proof of work in a past update. User "cryptonit" was sorry for the inconvenience caused. He listed key points to take into account:

- It was important for as many users as possible to secure the network via proof of stake minting.

- It was imperative for miners to mine via http://multipool.bit.diamonds/ instead of mining DMD directly. The total number of DMD pay outs had recently surpassed 10,000 on that site on the 10th September 2014.

- There was no hard fork or stuck network issue.

To the relief and joy of the community, a new mandatory Windows wallet client (version 2.0.4) update was made available at 21:49:14 UTC on the 20th September. User "cryptonit" reiterated the importance of not mining Diamond directly until block number 577,850 had been reached.

In the very early hours of the 28th September, block number 577,850 finally timestamped. There had been high anticipation from the community for proof of work mining to recommence. The first proof of work block, after PoW reactivation, was successfully found at block number 577,852 on the same day.

Block #577,850 (Reward 0.49178 DMD) September 28th 2014 at 00:50:28 AM UTC

Block #577,852 (Reward 1.05 DMD) September 28th 2014 at 01:16:31 AM UTC

On the 30th September, a non-profit project called Diamond Cloudmining went live at https://cloudmining.bit.diamonds/. Still active today, it's a supportive method to generate buy pressure in, and increase liquidity of, the DMD markets. DMD Cloudmining shares can be bought with Bitcoin and users get paid regularly in DMD. Ultimately, it adds security to the proof of stake mechanism of the network. On the official Diamond website, it is described as:

"Diamond Cloud Mining is a network support scheme where supporters are granted regular, hassle free, forever flowing stream of Diamonds. It's easy, it's profitable and makes power bills a thing of the past."

During the last three months of 2014, progress was quiet with hardly no major milestones. Two events which occurred were:

- A suggestion was made to change the timestamping algorithm from PoW/PoS. User "cryptonit" was not prepared to change it at the time.

- On the 15th December, Cryptsy initiated the DMD/XRP trading pair.

As is visible below, the market capitalisation did not surpass US$500,000 during 2014. An all time high for 2014 was recorded at US$409,074 on the 5th January according to www.coinmarketcap.com. The last recorded market capitalisation of 2014 was approximately US$140,000 (one DMD unit of account at ~US$0.18).

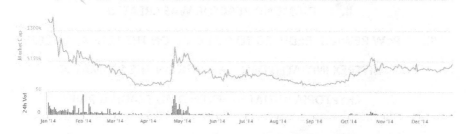

The last block timestamped (extracted by danbi's) to the blockchain in 2014 was:

Block #721,402 (Reward 1.05 DMD) December 31st 2014 at 11:59:43 PM UTC

I.   COMKORT INITIATED FOUR DMD TRADING PAIRS

II.   DIAMOND REACTOR WAS CREATED

III.   PoW REWARD REDUCED TO 0.21 DMD ON THE 12TH APRIL 2015

IV.   BITTREX INITIATED DMD TRADING ON THE 1ST MAY 2015

V.   CRYPTOPIA INITIATED SEVEN DMD TRADING PAIRS

5

PROOF OF WORK
BLOCK REWARD REDUCED

"If your actions inspire others to dream more, learn more, do more and become more, you are a leader.""

As is tradition in some parts of the world, New Year's resolutions had been made to change undesired habits. Members of the Diamond community were assessing previous successes and planning new innovative goals going forward. Both the DMD Multipool and Cloudmining services were still active as well as an ongoing press release campaign which had raised about 0.95 BTC so far.

As can be seen below, pay outs from the DMD Multipool had been frequent from the 22nd July 2014 to the 31st December 2014.

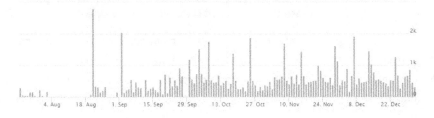

Besides active trading on other exchanges, another exchange added Diamond to their platform on the 13th January 2015. Comkort initiated four DMD related trading pairs without prior contact from the DMD Foundation. These were:

http://comkort.com/market/trade/dmd_usd
http://comkort.com/market/trade/dmd_btc
http://comkort.com/market/trade/dmd_ltc
http://comkort.com/market/trade/dmd_doge

Comkort opened for beta testing on the 20th February 2014 and went fully operational on the 1st March 2014. It was based in Tallinn, Estonia. It closed its doors on the 20th July 2015, three weeks after trading ceased. This gave its customers ample time to withdraw their coins.

Over the past few months, the number of DMD units of account mined/minted had fallen behind schedule of the initially planned coin rollout (not all DMD had been staking in user's personal wallets, especially coins held on exchanges). As a means to help raise the coin generation, user "popshot" posted details of the "Diamond Reactor Pre-launch Announcement" on the 28th January. In simple terms, the Diamond Reactor was originally described as a special wallet address (a service, not a personal client) that stakes Diamond at four times the normal rate (200% p.a.). It is therefore a way to increase the number of DMD via proof of stake.

However, the reactor was not created as initially planned. Parts of the community were against it. It went live as a normal proof of stake wallet address (50% p.a.). DMD donated to the reactor would help to support DMD Cloudmining as well as to pay holders varying amounts of DMD twice per month.

To summarise, the key reasons for the reactor were as follows:

- To help stick to the original coin rollout plan as much as possible.

- To provide hassle free stake to slot holders who want to see the long term success of the Diamond project.

- To secure the network with a larger generation of staked DMD units of account. This would reduce the risk (increase the cost) of future proof of stake attacks. It would also keep buy pressure strong on the exchanges.

The reactor went live straight away and supporters of Diamond were quick to take advantage of the service. A logo had been proposed for the Diamond Reactor:

DMD REACTOR

On the 18th February, over 100,000 DMD had already been redistributed from the DMD Multipool. At the time, this was above 10% of total generated coins. This had removed coins out of the market and into the pockets of investors who could, if they wished, stake at 50% p.a. The table below shows the top five DMD pay out days since the debut of http://multipool.bit.diamonds/ on the 22nd July 2014.

Date	Total DMD Pay Out
21st August 2014	2,798.07211400
2nd September 2014	2,040.49370700
7th December 2014	1,914.68469300
25th October 2014	1,868.44268300
8th October 2014	1,759.14562700

On the 23rd March at 23:40:07 UTC, user "cryptonit" notified the community that the first test runs of the next wallet release were complete. Further development of the code was planned. A promise was made to release the update early enough before the total number of DMD reached 1,000,000. He also instructed users, exchanges, mining pools and other services to update as soon as it became available. Several changes were going to take effect post coin total 1,000,000 DMD.

On the 8th April 2015 at 13:59:17 UTC, user "popshot" published details, and the relevant download links, of the awaited wallet release (version 2.0.5.5). Protocol changes to come into force post 1,000,000 coins included:

- Block reward reduction from 1.05 DMD to 0.21 DMD (80% less).

- Average time for both PoW and PoS blocks at 100 seconds.

- Minimum PoS time at three days (reduced from min seven days maturity).

On the 12th April 2015, the number of DMD units of account generated to date surpassed one million as soon as block number 877,395 timestamped:

Block #877,395 (Reward 95.502739 DMD) April 12th 2015 at 09:07:22 AM UTC

Described as a nice surprise by user "cryptonit", Bittrex activated the DMD/BTC trading pair on the 1st May 2015. One particular response was by user "pokeytex" who said:

"Well now. This totally went under the radar! Congratulations community!"

Bittrex was founded in Seattle, Washington, USA. It began operations on the 13th February 2014 in beta testing mode. Fifteen days later, the exchange went live. Bill Shihara is the co-founder and CEO of Bittrex. His team's mission is to continue to deliver one of the fastest and most secure trading platforms available.

Two months remained until the second anniversary of the blockchain. With a core team consisting of six individuals, there was sufficient work to be done. Funds raised (~2.23 BTC) from a recent press release initiative were still available to spend. User "popshot" suggested to use the funds to sponsor two articles, one article on CoinDesk, the other on CryptoCoinNews. This was not a certainty, so further ideas from the community were welcome.

On the 3rd June, live trading of Diamond, DMD, against seven separate cryptocurrencies commenced on Cryptopia. It is an exchange based in New Zealand. Cryptopia tweeted the news:

Cryptopia Exchange @Cryptopia_NZ · 3 Jun 2015
Diamond(DMD) Now live on Cryptopia
7 trade markets. BlockExplorer and MarketPlace
cryptopia.co.nz @dmdcoin
Welcome Home :)

Other events which occurred during this period were:

- A brand new block explorer was unveiled on the 19th January. It was situated at http://explorer.bit.diamonds/. It was noted, via the "Rich List" on that website, that the top 1,000 wallets held about 787,258 DMD (~96%).

- On the 12th May, user "popshot" was pleased to announce a refreshed version of the official website at https://bit.diamonds (see image below). It was by no means complete, but adequate for "public consumption".

I.   **SECOND ANNIVERSARY CAKE COMPETITION COMMENCED**

II.   **ALL TIME HIGH 2015 MARKET CAPITALISATION ATTAINED**

III.   **USER "HALLARED" WON THE 2015 CAKE COMPETITION**

IV.   **PRESS RELEASE INITIATIVES IMPLEMENTED**

V.   **OFFICIAL WEBSITE TRANSLATED INTO OTHER LANGUAGES**

6

DIAMOND SECOND YEAR ANNIVERSARY

"The longer you wait for something, the more you appreciate it when you get it, because anything worth having is definitely worth waiting for."

As the second anniversary of the DMD blockchain was on the horizon, user "cryptonit" wanted ideas from the community about how to celebrate it. On the 5th June 2015, user "mightgetlucky" simply stated "A cake?". It was only a matter of hours before a final decision was made. A decision was quickly made to proceed with the "2nd Anniversary Birthday Cake Competition". A deadline for entries was unsurprisingly the 13th July 2015. Rules were stated as follows:

- DMD Diamond written on the cake.

- Two lit candles on the cake.

- Photo of the cake besides Bitcointalk name written on a piece of paper.

A bounty of 200 DMD was available to the winner. This would later become 250 DMD thanks to the generosity of user "crazyivan".

On the 11th June 2015 at 22:12:17 UTC, user "popshot" was pleased Diamond was going to have its first proper premium level press release from PRBuzz. Diamond was going to be featured on major news, industry and social media sites. The funds of 2.23 BTC raised fell short (US$511), so an additional amount of US$288 came from the DMD Foundation team.

Four days later, an article titled "2 Years in Development Valuable Bitcoin Alternative Diamond Coin (DMD) Offers 50% Annual Interest" was published on a myriad of websites (see pages 94 and 95 of the appendix).

On the 23rd June, the 1,000,000th block was successfully timestamped:

Block #1,000,000 (Reward 0.21 DMD) June 23rd 2015 at 04:55:29 PM UTC

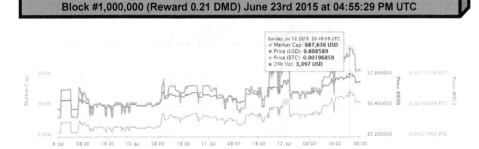

On the 6th July 2015, the Diamond market capitalisation surpassed US$500,000 for the first time since the 19th December 2013. This recent surge above US$500,000 attracted new faces to the community as well as more frequent posts submitted to the official Diamond Bitcointalk thread.

Six days later, the 2015 ATH market capitalisation at US$687,636 was recorded according to data derived from www.coinmarketcap.com. A corresponding value per DMD unit of account of US$0.608589 or 196,859 Bitcoin Satoshi stood.

Date	Low US$	Open US$	Close US$	High US$	Volume US$	Market Cap US$
10th July	0.403463	0.410907	0.475378	0.493534	1,376	462,939
11th July	0.418426	0.475166	0.557441	0.558386	2,548	535,971
12th July	0.464333	0.568794	0.555296	0.608589	3,123	642,137

On the 13th July 2015, the "2nd Anniversary Birthday Cake Competition" ended. User "cryptonit" at 18:09:55 UTC gave thanks to everyone who had participated. He admitted it had been difficult to select the winner.

First place went to user "hallared" who won 250 DMD. When he submitted his entry (1) on the 12th July at 18:56:30 UTC, he said "Happy Birthday DMD Diamond! I would like to congratulate and thank DMD Diamond, the Dev Team and all community members for 2 marvellous years. To honour the memorable day, July 13th 2015, I made this delicious birthday cake in advance."

Second place went to user "stoody" who won 50 DMD. It was submitted (2) on the 1st July at 02:47:50 UTC. He said: "here is my entire into the bday cake comp...". User "crazyivan" was so impressed with the entry from user "stoody" that he personally increased the original first prize 200 DMD bounty to 250 DMD.

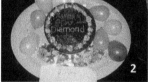

Third place went to user "jepistons" who won 20 DMD. It was submitted (3) on the 6th July. He said: "its called Confetti Birthday Cake even the letters on the cake are edible"

Assessed as a great success, the community anticipated a similar competition next year. Users "crazyivan", "vagnavs", "chilo", "hallared" and others congratulated the winners and wished Diamond a happy second birthday.

The last block (PoS) timestamped before the second year ended was block number 1,032,675. The next block was also proof of stake (see below).

Block #1,032,675 (Reward 0.989041 DMD) July 13th 2015 at 06:21:01 AM UTC

Block #1,032,676 (Reward 0.357534 DMD) July 13th 2015 at 06:24:23 AM UTC

On the 27th July 2015, an article was published on an independent news website at http://bitcoinlasvegas.net by someone known as Vegasguy titled "Diamond Coin (DMD) One of the Best Coins in Crypto! $600,000 Market Cap. Strong steady Climb! 2 Years Old!". The article predominantly consisted of images which celebrated the ongoing success of Diamond.

Motivated by the success of the previous press release initiative, user "popshot" was eager to proceed with another. Persistence was important, in his opinion, as a way to attract more attention from those who had not yet seen, heard or read the previous press release. In the second release, user "popshot" promised to match each and every contribution made by each supporter. He wanted to begin the press release immediately after the fund goal had been met. There was plenty of news to write about.

On the 27th August at 23:14:15 UTC, user "popshot" said:

> *"I think crypto economy is struggling only in the eyes of people obsessed with numbers and charts.*

> *Let us not forget that these are the early days of this industry. It's still very small making it incredibly volatile.*

> *We are building foundations here and truly successful project is a marathon not a sprint!"*

On the 7th September, an article was published thanks to the PR Initiative above. A total of 2.27 BTC raised made it a reality. The article titled "How Anyone Can Make Money With Digital Currency: Bitcoin Alternative DMD Explains" can be found in the appendix of this book on pages 96 and 97.

On the 26th November, a couple of Diamond promotional banners were unveiled:

Other events which occurred included:

- On the 10th July, the DMD Cloudmining project had redistributed over 100,000 DMD between its shareholders.

- On the 16th July, Cryptsy initiated the DMD/CAD trading pair.

- On the 21st July, the Russian version of the official Diamond website went live at http://bit.diamonds/index-ru.html.

- On the 4th August, the Chinese version of the official Diamond website went live at http://bit.diamonds/index-cn.html.

- On the 9th August, thanks to Systh, Diamond got its own "flat web icon". User "popshot" was impressed (see images below).

- On the 22nd September, a cloud staking service called Staisybit added DMD.

- On the 14th October, a brand new DMD block explorer went live at http://dmd.presstab.pw.

- On the 21st November, the Japanese version of the official Diamond website went live. Praise was given to @moritakitsune for providing it.

Diamond   Diamond
cc-DMD   cc-DMD-alt

I.   **LEGENDARY TEN AUCTIONS BEGAN ON THE 10TH DECEMBER 2015**

II.   **PROOF OF STAKE REWARD REDUCED FROM 50% TO 25% p.a.**

III.   **TEN LEGENDARY WINNERS OF THE UCAs ANNOUNCED**

IV.   **VERSION 2.1.0.1 WALLET CLIENT RELEASED ON THE 10TH MAY 2016**

V.   **BITTREX BECAME THE ONLY EXCHANGE TRADING DMD**

7

LEGENDARY TEN

"Investment in Legendary 10 address asset is not only an investment in personal gain but also an investment in security, development and stability of the wider network that will back value of DMD Diamond investors' portfolios for years to come." - user "crazyivan"

Following on from a delay to give people ample time to prepare and spread the word, the DMD Foundation created an innovative and unique project called "Legendary Ten" on the 10th December 2015. Ten special wallet addresses, named after some of the most precious natural diamonds in the world, became available to purchase with BTC via auction. Core foundation members were initially barred from bidding, but would be permitted to buy any address, which failed to sell, at the minimum bid. To begin with, the first legendary diamonds ready for auction at http://bitdiamonds/auction.html were "The Allnatt Diamond" and "The Moussaieff Diamond" during phase one. All three auction phases were as follows:

Phase 1 | 2 Unique Legendary 10 Crypto Assets | 10 December 2015 - 24 December 2015

Phase 2 | 3 Unique Legendary 10 Crypto Assets | 24 December 2015 - 16 January 2016

Phase 3 | 5 Unique Legendary 10 Crypto Assets | 16 January 2016 - 06 February 2016

In addition to the number of auctioned unique crypto assets (UCAs) increasing as one phase ended and the next one began, the Bitcoin starting bid for each would be higher. One reason for this decision was to compensate for early winners waiting longer than others for the auction process to end. Three methods by which people could bid were via the official DMD Forum, by private messaging users "cryptonit" or "popshot" on Bitcointalk, or via the auction site. Other rules which applied were:

- A bid must exceed the previous bid by at least 0.1 BTC and a maximum bid (kept secret from others) can be submitted.

- Auction winners must pay the total Bitcoin amount a few days after the auction ended, otherwise the second highest bidder becomes able to claim.

- One legendary ten address per individual. No exceptions.

Each legendary ten unique crypto asset winner would have a choice of two options:

1. A wallet with a 3,000 DMD holding limit with 2x stake multiplier.

2. A wallet with a 15,000 DMD holding limit with a 1.25x stake multiplier.

Once chosen, the winner had to provide his/her wallet address to which the stake boost would apply. They also had the right to personalise the address with a name and a 144 text message (both enshrined forever). However, if the owner wished to transfer the UCA, these would disappear. Some other benefits of the UCAs are:

- Ten strong staking nodes increase the security of the network.

- Owner feels epic holding a rare, unique crypto asset.

- All raised Bitcoin went entirely to DMD Development.

- Holders can attract the attention of outside individuals or groups.

- The UCAs withdraw substantial coins (up to 150,000 DMD) from the market.

- Overall staked generation of DMD increased towards scheduled rollout plan.

As well as the beginning of the legendary ten auctions, a roadmap of future short, mid and long term goals was published. Short term goals were mainly aimed at making the wallet client software more user friendly in relation to proof of stake management. Mid terms goals included plans to create an Android Wallet with staking ability and a more professional looking wallet client GUI (Graphical User Interface). Over the longer term, merchant, escrow, smart contract functionality and other services were set goals.

Date	Low US$	Open US$	Close US$	High US$	Volume US$	Market Cap US$
31st Dec	0.315514	0.328812	0.338348	0.347821	518	479,171
1st Jan	0.309551	0.338371	0.349083	0.349284	1,696	493,757

On the last day of 2015, the market capitalisation was recorded at US$493,723 according to www.coinmarketcap.com. This was a yearly increase of roughly 250% on last year's figure of US$140,704. In addition, the price of one DMD unit of account had risen from US$0.180733 to US$0.338348 (87.2% increase). The chart below displays Diamond market capitalisation throughout the year of 2015:

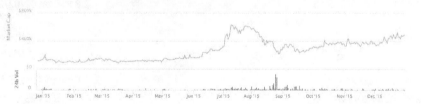

On the 16th January, phase two ended. Two of the four (one Diamond rolled over from phase one) diamonds in phase two sold. The two unsold diamonds went into phase three (seven auctioned). Due to not being sold in time, user "cryptonit" bought the "Heart of Eternity" Diamond for 2.4 BTC (also aided the funding goal).

Three days later, the number of DMD generated since the very first block surpassed 1,500,000. This marked the time when the proof of stake reward reduced from 50% to 25% p.a. This change occurred at the following block:

Block #1,349,953 (Reward 0.916438 DMD) January 19th 2016 at 12:57:44 PM UTC

On the 19th January 2016, Cryptsy issued an article in which they submitted a list of cryptocurrencies which were available for users to withdraw their coins. User "cryptonit" utterly insisted anyone with DMD units of account there to immediately withdraw them. Cryptsy's official website at www.cryptsy.com went down soon after. There were, unfortunately, some people who did not manage to withdraw all their coins. Months of silence and legal activity followed.

In February, all ten unique crypto asset auctions ended. What follows are all ten assets with corresponding winners, winning bids and auction end dates:

De Beers Centenary Diamond

Won by "Brian" for 2.8 BTC on 09/02/2016

The Cullinan Diamond

Won by "Alex" for 2.8 BTC on 08/02/2016

The Hope Diamond

Won by "crowetic" for 2.8 BTC on 09/02/2016

The Sancy Diamond

Won by "florinb" for 2.8 BTC on 02/02/2016

The Allnatt Diamond

Won by "alaoa" for 2.6 BTC on 20/12/2015

Koh-I-Noor Diamond

Won by "alba77" for 3.0 BTC on 25/01/2016

The Moussaieff Red Diamond

Won by "BogdanCo" for 2.0 BTC on 15/01/2016

Wittelsbach Diamond

Won by "pazor" for 2.4 BTC on 25/01/2016

The Heart of Eternity Diamond

Won by "cryptonit " for 2.4 BTC on 15/01/2016

The Steinmetz Pink Diamond

Won by "kishore" for 2.4 BTC on 30/01/2016

Proceeding several months of development, on the 8th May 2016 at 19:17:41 UTC, user "cryptonit" notified the community that beta testing of the next wallet update had been successful. Finally, there had been no detectable issues found.

Two days later, user "popshot" announced the release of version 2.1.0.1 of the Windows (Mac OS X released on the 13th May) wallet client software. He described the release as long awaited, complicated and mandatory. It was primarily devoted to the holders of the ten unique crypto assets. Funds raised from the UCA had helped "push the sails of the DMD Diamond ship to the new seas of opportunity and development". He emphasised the importance of mining pools, exchanges and regular users to update before block number 1,549,200. The proof of work coin support share (0.01 DMD) would no longer exist. It would be replaced with a coin support stake boosted address for similar effect.

On the 14th May 2016, the scheduled changes to the network kicked in. It was recommended for legendary ten holders to wait at least one day before staking due to technical constraints. A total of 1,612,535.49564241 DMD had been mined/minted so far. Block number 1,549,200 was:

Block #1,549,200 (Reward 0.2 DMD) May 14th 2016 at 05:45:47 AM UTC

On the 29th May 2016, Cryptopia warned the Diamond community of their plans to close all DMD trading pairs on their platform. Users were told to withdraw all their DMD units of account before the 5th June 2016. As a result, Bittrex would become the only recognised exchange offering live Diamond trading.

I.   VERSION 2.1.0.3 WALLET CLIENTS RELEASED ON THE 8TH JUNE 2016

II.   NORMAL PoS INCREASED TO 30% P.A. FOR ONE MONTH

III.   3RD ANNIVERSARY CAKE COMPETITION WINNERS ANNOUNCED

IV.   USER "POPSHOT" ADDRESSED THE COMMUNITY

V.   DIAMOND MARKET CAPITALISATION HAD INCREASED BY 1,100%

8

DIAMOND THIRD YEAR ANNIVERSARY

"On July 13, 2016, we'll be celebrating the 3rd anniversary of DMD Diamond. Each such event is special, because it's a testament to community's commitment and dedication to make DMD Diamond a fantastic vehicle for prosperity." - user "popshot"

For the past few weeks, the developers had been busy fixing the code after they noticed that the Legendary Ten stake boosts were not working properly. An updated wallet client (version 2.1.0.3) was therefore released, on the 8th June 2016, to solve this issue. This update was mandatory and had to be installed before a hard fork set at 12:00 UTC on the 19th June 2016. Unique crypto asset holders eagerly awaited for this to take effect.

Another feature had also been implemented into the next update. A temporary boost to the normal proof of stake rate from 25% to 30% p.a. for one month beginning on the 19th June 2016. The developers were proud of the achievements made and wanted each and every investor in the project to feel the same.

On the 11th June, version 2.1.0.3 of the Mac OS X wallet client became available. Special thanks were given to user "davembg" who compiled it.

In much the same way to the previous year, a cake competition began on the 22nd June 2016. Last year's competition was a great success. This year's entries were expected to be better. A precious cake (photo) was sought after:

- Three lit candles on top of the cake.

- DMD Diamond clearly written on the cake.

- Entries name written on a piece of paper besides the cake.

First prize was set at 233 DMD and a free Diamond reactor slot. Second and third

prizes were 66 DMD and 33 DMD respectively. Participants had about three weeks to gain inspiration from last year's entries and then bake a grand cake.

On the 13th July, user "popshot" was excited to announce the winners of the "3rd Anniversary DMD Diamond Birthday Bake Off". He thanked all participants who had produced excellent cakes.

First prize (1) went to user "hallared" who submitted a strawberry filled blue marzipan cake on the 12th July. He wished the DMD Team and the community members all the best for the upcoming year.

Second place went to user "shinydiamond" who submitted his entry on the 11th July. He said "Me and my sunshine gave a go and made the cake. We were so eager to eat it we forgot to place a card with a name".

Third place went to user "wiser" who submitted two cake versions on the 8th July. It was a gluten free vanilla cake mixed cake (Pamela is the brand). The frosting was cream cheese frosting. The diamonds on the cake were made of marzipan almond candy.

To coincide with the third anniversary of the DMD blockchain, user "popshot" submitted an extensive post in which he assessed the progress made so far. Three years had passed since the first block timestamped at 06:22:11 UTC on the 13th July 2013. He acknowledged the tireless and relentless work of many people who had contributed to the journey so far. Notable successes included:

- The hashing algorithm changed from Scrypt to Groestl (April 2014).

- DMD Cloudmining continued to maintain buying pressure in the markets and, as a result, increased the value of each and every DMD unit of account (September 2014)

- Diamond reactor had increased the security of the network (January 2015)

- Legendary Ten was a special, innovative occasion that bestowed ten ultra rare digital diamonds (February 2016)

He was proud to describe how the DMD team (people with real lives) had forged strong relationships with other parties. He viewed this as a vital way to expose Diamond to a wider audience, either inside or outside the crypto sphere.

User "popshot" also touched upon a future overhaul of the code base, version 3.0, in the not so distant future. An upgrade to the most promising parts of the BTC code, but more advanced. He was looking forward to the release.

Block number 1,649,646 signified three years since the birth of the blockchain:

Block #1,649,646 (Reward 0.2 DMD) July 13th 2016 at 06:22:11 AM UTC

On the 19th August 2016, a video titled "bit.diamonds | WHAT IS YOUR CHOICE?" was uploaded to YouTube. It describes the benefits and coin specification of Diamond. Ultimately, it promotes Diamond as a rare and secure investment. A screenshot from the video (see below) presents six main characteristics:

From September 2014 (the month in which the DMD Cloudmining initiative was born) to September 2016, the market capitalisation of DMD increased by roughly 1,100%. One unit of DMD account also increased by roughly 400%. Figures tabulated below are derived from historical data on www.coinmarketcap.com.

Date	Low	Open	Close	High	Volume	Market Cap
2014						
5th Sept	0.058137	0.064567	0.058494	0.064567	82	37,105
12th Sept	0.062177	0.076242	0.062976	0.076401	93	44,684
19th Sept	0.064307	0.069832	0.084093	0.090236	382	41,513
26th Sept	0.072309	0.073278	0.080914	0.085327	103	43,759
2016						
5th Sept	0.290448	0.304512	0.293455	0.306020	233	530,516
12th Sept	0.296706	0.331742	0.313429	0.331898	455	580,905
19th Sept	0.269580	0.302985	0.279588	0.306922	1,669	533,169
26th Sept	0.274729	0.288396	0.282282	0.296877	176	509,909

During the last few months of 2016, there were not many major events which took place. Work continued to get Diamond on to a second exchange, namely Livecoin. Diamond had been fluctuating on Livecoin's voting list of potential coin additions between first and third position. Other cryptocurrencies in contention for first place were NEM and Factom. Bittrex remained the sole exchange on which live Diamond trades were occurring.

Other events which occurred during this period included:

- On the 8th July, wallet client updates (version 2.1.0.4) for Window and Mac OS X were made available. Installation was not a mandatory requirement, but recommended for users who had been having trouble syncing the blockchain. Two weeks later, user "cryptonit" insisted all users had to update.

- On the 14th July, user "hallared" began a "Diamond Strawberry Guessing Contest".

- On the 8th December, @CryptoArtEvent on Twitter was happy to announce that Diamond would sponsor the #CryptoArtGallery in Manchester UK.

As can be seen below, the last block timestamped to the DMD blockchain was block number 1,940,688 via proof of stake. A total of 1,892,570.73839741 DMD had been mined/minted since block number one.

Block #1,940,688 (Reward 0.189041 DMD) December 31st 2016 at 11:59:23 PM UTC

I.   DMD MARKET CAP AT US$414,000 ON THE 1ST JANUARY 2017

II.   MARKET CAP SURPASSED US$1,000,000 ON THE 3RD APRIL 2017

III.   PRICE OF ONE DMD SURPASSED US$1 ON THE 19TH MAY 2017

IV.   ALL TIME HIGH MARKET CAP ATTAINED (BEFORE V3 BLOCKCHAIN)

V.   THIRD YEAR ANNIVERSARY CELEBRATED ON THE 13TH JULY 2017

9

MARKET CAPITALISATION
BEGAN TO SURGE

"We are excited about the future and feel that DMD Diamond is on the path to become a strong and recognizable monetary system on the cryptocurrency market that empowers people to achieve financial freedom" - DMD Foundation

For the first time since the 6th January 2014, the US Dollar price of 1 Bitcoin surpassed 1,000 on the 1st January 2017. Despite this, the market capitalisation of Diamond had been decreasing. Bittrex was the only recognised exchange on which live trading of DMD was occurring. User "cryptonit" thought it was a golden time to buy DMD. What follows are the US Dollar figures of Diamond and the top performing cryptocurrencies on the 1st January 2017:

	Low US$	Open US$	Close US$	High US$	Volume US$	Market Cap US$
Bitcoin	958.70	963.66	998.33	1,003.08	147,775,000	15,491,200,000
Ethereum	7.98	7.98	8.17	8.47	14,731,700	698,149,000
Litecoin	4.33	4.33	4.51	4.52	11,337,500	212,691,000
Diamond	0.149685	0.219242	0.149706	0.219274	3,152	414,930

Some people were showing signs of agitation at the fall in DMD market capitalisation. Others enthusiastically said it was a great opportunity to buy cheap DMD. On the 18th January 2017, user "cryptonit" notified the community that the market capitalisation had more than doubled over the past seven days:

Date	1 DMD US$	1 DMD BTC Satoshi	24h Volume US$	Market Cap US$
11th January 2017	0.155204	20,110	57	296,180
18th January 2017	0.332652	37,888	1,854	637,790

On the 1st March, user "cryptonit" was happy to reiterate the importance of the legendary ten wallet addresses. Bitcoin raised continued to help enormously with the development of DMD V3. All ten wallet addresses on this day were:

The Heart of Eternity	dasHERZmwgtvWGNRxs55GPrXsAKwY7bX85
The Cullinan	dEB799gGhnG89b8bkcPUitgXiJWc7ggNCM
Koh-I-Noor	dMdjuF7xcsUvkYy2ikaQkx5z5viqNvhzxz
The Allnatt	dTKsf6qD7BeVN7bNZpBM2M1iXfbrt5vvak
The Steinmetz Pink	dW4mnJLQZwFExTBFTBdGSNte71TfvqC8LX
De Beers Centenary	dTuJJvYoDcerBaHwoK8cK2oEEpYEWr8Tdh
The Moussaieff Red	dMbc7KM7cDy487C9FrWwvyaquprTgtCWZ8
The Sancy	dJWVbYhykxPwJQ1PxxjtQjBoGc1abhfQh7
Wittelsbach	dFKNwDWexXFapBBxRh5FsYtj3GkG8TyS75
The Hope	dZTEMvLjwWjtiH3k1LCCX2soLXhQcUDLyZ

All legendary ten holders were reminded about their premium access to help from the development team. If anybody discovered an empty legendary ten wallet address, they were encouraged to contact the holder if they wanted it instead.

As soon as the block below timestamped, a total of 2,000,000 DMD had been generated to date. User "cryptonit" was glad to still be part of Diamond.

Block #2,075,320 (Reward 14.452054 DMD) March 23rd 2017 at 12:04:10 AM UTC

Cryptocurrency followers and enthusiasts are aware of how quickly the market capitalisation of coins can change. A key milestone was reached on the 3rd April 2017, a date on which the market capitalisation of Diamond surpassed US$1,000,000 for the first time. As can be seen below, the price of one unit of DMD account went over US$0.50 for the first time since the end of July 2015.

Date	Low US$	Open US$	Close US$	High US$	Volume US$	Market Cap US$
3rd Jan	0.136432	0.153119	0.174883	0.177023	1,689	290,160
17th Jan	0.224304	0.228032	0.248287	0.258071	232	436,892
31st Jan	0.300735	0.300735	0.318439	0.325184	198	581,133
14th Feb	0.278587	0.286286	0.286587	0.292282	1,082	558,135
28th Feb	0.212380	0.215038	0.213710	0.224498	227	423,544
14th Mar	0.246031	0.250991	0.248012	0.259759	174	499,153
28th Mar	0.331409	0.347488	0.383675	0.417054	5,730	697,409
3rd Apr	0.407152	0.440912	0.560210	0.623678	16,512	889,945
4th Apr	0.408733	0.560970	0.476857	0.562272	8,810	1,135,110

The 3rd April 2017 was described as a great day for DMD investors by user "popshot". He said it looked like just the beginning and anticipated more growth in the near future. He praised those who had supported the project for years. He also encouraged further feedback, engagement and expertise from the community.

Another update about DMD V3 was released. He repeated that it would be a complete overhaul of the code, not a simple code adjustment. As the changes were going to be so profound, the branding would have to change too. A strong emphasis remained on security and stability which had to be higher. User "popshot" mentioned masternode technology:

"A concept that has been time tested and is safe to implement and build upon. In the initial phase Master Nodes will allow for instant and more anonymous transactions. However, there's much more that could be and would be done and many of you have already expressed in this thread further potential uses of this technology."

As part of the first sneak peak of DMD V3 (implementation of masternodes, MN) in the next update, a new single colour and flat version of the DMD logo was unveiled on the 24th April 2017. They had aimed to make it compatible with the old logo while at the same time making sure the old logo can be used too. It was not going to fully replace the old branding.

On the 7th May, the DMD Foundation published "DMD Diamond Newsletter 05/2017" in which they covered recent progress. They were happy about the recent "organic growth" of the market capitalisation over the preceding several months. A growing number of people were discovering cryptocurrencies and blockchain technology. A quote from the newsletter was as follows:

"We will see many improvements to the protocol not only in terms of security, speed and privacy, but the new code base of DMD V3 will facilitate the use of Diamond Masternodes. The new Diamond Masternode network will form a cornerstone of future projects scheduled for 2018 that will add to the value of the coin."

During May, the value of one unit of DMD account continued to increase. Many in the community expected to see parity with the US Dollar very soon. Since the 23rd January 2014, the value had remained below US$1. On the 9th May, the value was slightly shy at US$0.995, but failed to surpass. At roughly 8 UTC on the 19th May, it did exceed US$1.

Another price milestone happened on the 6th June 2017. According to historical data derived from www.coinmarketcap.com, the price of one DMD unit of account attained its highest ever value at US$2.78. This broke the last all time high set at US$2.76 on the 19th December 2013.

On the 22nd June 2017, DMD Diamond's 4th Anniversary Birthday Cake Competition began. It had become a customary tradition for the community. As was the case previously, the winners were going to be announced on the 13th July 2017. Prizes were as follows:

- 1st prize—Silver DMD Anniversary coin and chance to win a 10,000 DMD MN

- 2nd prize—100 DMD

- 3rd prize—50 DMD

On the 28th June 2017, the all time high market capitalisation (before the end of the old V2 blockchain) was attained. It quickly ascended to a recorded market capitalisation at about US$19,106,393. Volume had also sky rocketed to millions of US$ on the sole exchange on which DMD trading was happening. One unit of DMD account reached a high of US$8.84. A chart derived from www.coinmarketcap.com clearly shows the ascent:

Historical figures from www.coinmarketcap.com show how quickly the value of one DMD unit of account ascended on the 28th June 2017:

Date	Low US$	Open US$	Close US$	High US$	Volume US$	Market Cap US$
27th June	2.59	2.90	2.84	2.92	21,258	6,259,760
28th June	2.75	2.90	5.79	8.84	4,345,100	6,271,370

On the 13th July, it was time to celebrate four years since the Diamond blockchain launched. Twelve lustrous cakes had been baked, prepared and entered into the competition. For the third time running, user "hallared" won first prize (1). He won a silver ounze DMD 4th anniversary coin (not yet released) and a 1 in 85 chance to win a 10,000 DMD Masternode.

Two entries won second place (2 and 3). Both users "emmytim" and "yelena" each received 100 DMD.

Taking into account the number and quality of entries compared to past years, further rewards were made. Entries (4) and (5) submitted by, respectively, users "dassjsk" and "diamond_masieeka" each received 10 DMD.

Seven other entries to the competition submitted each received 4 DMD. All cakes were beautiful, so the DMD Foundation felt rewarding each entry was appropriate.

1.   Extrawelt

2.   BB2EBB

3.   Haller

4.   Kitkat

5.   Capricoinn

6.   Hsbookworm

7.   Carface

As can be seen below, the last block timestamped to the DMD blockchain during the fourth year was block number 2,263,056. A total of 2,182,232.91993974 DMD had been generated since the first block. The next block timestamped via proof of work mining.

Block #2,263,056 (Reward 0.633561 DMD) July 13th 2017 at 06:21:07 AM UTC

Block #2,263,057 (Reward 0.2 DMD) July 13th 2017 at 06:23:02 AM UTC

Supporters of Diamond publicly wished the cryptocurrency a happy birthday. Eight well wishes were:

alba77

"HAPPY 4TH ANNIVERSARY DMD DIAMOND. May you all live long and prosper."

carface

"Happy birthday Diamond DMD! Really exciting times!!"

crazyivan

"Let me join Bday party. Best wishes to DMD Diamond and all members of the DMD community. May good health, great women and awesome prices follow us in the future. Happy Bday DMD."

extrawelt

"Happy Birthday Diamond DMD!"

Limx Dev

"Happy Birthday Diamond!!"

pokeytex

"Happy Birthday DMD! Congratulations to the entire community!"

shveicar

"Happy birthday to the DMD community! 4 years is the great time for crypto currency. And Diamond today has a solid foundation for further progress."

Telescopium

"Happy birthday to the DMD community. Now I managed to accumulate 2500 DMD, tell me that I already be a wealthy man in the near future?"

Other events which occurred during this period were:

- On the 6th January, user "cryptonit" started a small competition called the "Summer Price Guess Event". Entrants had to estimate the US$ price of one single Bitcoin on the 21st June 2017 within a US100 range. Entrants also had to send 100 DMD to a specific DMD wallet address. The winner was "Limx Dev" who guessed US$2,100-2,200. He received all DMD entrance fees.

- On the 15th January, both the DMD Multipool and Cloudmining services combined had redistributed over 300,000 DMD.

- On the 1st March, the top two Diamond wallet address were the Reactor and Bittrex containing 98,755 DMD and 73,194 DMD respectively.

- On the 9th April, the Crypto Art Gallery Event took place in Manchester, UK.

- On the 4th May, the "4th Anniversary DMD Silver Coin" was first mentioned. A prototype image was published (see bottom left).

- On the 15th May, a final decision was made not to implement proof of work timestamping in DMD V3.

- On the 12th June, a photo of a wooden box for holding the fourth anniversary coins was unveiled (see bottom right).

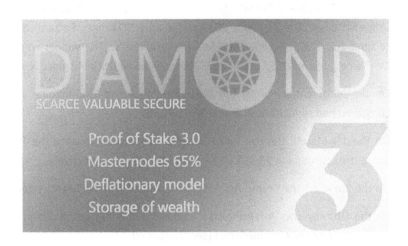

I.   DIAMOND V3 WHITEPAPER PUBLISHED ON THE 13TH JULY 2017

II. TESTNET MADE PUBLIC TO EVERYONE ON THE 19TH AUGUST 2017

III. ONE DMD INCREASED IN VALUE BY OVER 2,000%

IV. LAST BLOCK OF V2 TIMESTAMPED ON 13TH SEPTEMBER 2017

V.   FIRST BLOCK OF V3 TIMESTAMPED ON 14TH SEPTEMBER 2017

10

TRANSITION TO NEW DMD V3 BLOCKCHAIN

"Thank you to all the people, both DMD Diamond Foundation members and fantastic Diamond Community, who have contributed with their input to this document and support over the years which inspired us to move forward and continue to develop DMD Diamond with passion." - DMD Foundation

To remain strong, competitive and robust, the DMD Foundation published a whitepaper detailing reasons for the transition to a new blockchain. Three primary contributors to the document were users "cryptonit", "popshot" and "Limx Dev". Other community members had also had their input.

Diamond DMD Version 3 (DMD V3) had been in progress for quite some time. Key information initially given in the whitepaper was about the new coin specification:

- Total coin cap remains unchanged at 4.38 million, but generation of DMD gradually decreases over time.

- Block time is average 135 seconds (without Masternode)

- Initial block reward of 0.0235 DMD to give time for users to transition to new blockchain (2.35 DMD reward shortly after, then decreases over time).

Transition to New DMD V3 Blockchain

A major shift from hybrid PoW/PoS to sole PoS was scheduled to take place in two months time. Active staking nodes and Masternodes (MN) would serve to confirm transactions and secure the network. Stakers and masternode holders would, in total, receive 35% and 65% respectively of block rewards.

A more advanced version of proof of stake (PoS 3.0) was being developed to address the underlying issues present in the current (PoS 2.0) model. In version two, proof of stake was providing very little incentive to users who kept their nodes (computers) running continuously. Many were disconnecting from the network for long periods, gaining enough "coin age" and then connecting again to claim their rewards. This meant fewer active nodes, therefore more risk of network attack. Proof of stake 3.0 would only allow active participants chance to get a share of the block reward.

Another method to acquire DMD units of account would be via the introduction of masternodes. They are constantly connected computers (active nodes) which allow their users, who get rewarded regularly, to perform bespoke services. Other cryptocurrencies developed and implemented these as a way to make sure enough nodes remained active. To receive a masternode, users must:

- Send exactly 10,000 DMD in a MN ready wallet address. This number also proves the holder has a right to be a DMD network service provider (MN).

- Leave the 10,000 DMD as untouched collateral.

Two services would be up and running from the offset of DMD V3:

- QuickTX - this features sends DMD fully confirmed in a few seconds.

- MixTX - increases the anonymity of transaction by making it more difficult to trace source address from which the coins were sent.

As a special case, the DMD Foundation will have five masternodes and each legendary ten holder will receive one masternode (instead of receiving a stake bonus). Coins cannot be moved or spent from these fifteen masternodes.

There would be times at which running a masternode is more rewarding than staking, and vice versa. If too many masternodes exist, the reward share for each would be too low. People would then shift to staking. A quote from the DMD V3 Whitepaper describes this as follows:

"This is self-adjusting system, profit driven, that makes sure Diamond Network will never be without Proof of Stake securing it and never be without enough Masternodes to guarantee smooth working of Diamond Network services."

On the 29th July, user "cryptonit" posted an update on the current development of DMD V3. Several alpha testnet versions wee being extensively tested. The DMD Foundation did not want to put a definite date on the final release, but were driven to make sure the code worked properly. User "shveicar" said the following:

"It's best to check everything attentively and carefully before publishing a version in which there may be errors."

Bounties were available to write technical guides for software users. People had to private message the DMD Foundation with links to previous guides written. Two people per bounty accepted (winner get 90% follow up attempt get 10% of bounty)

On the 19th August 2017, the DMD Foundation made a decision to make testing of DMD V3 public to everyone on testnet without invites (invites were initially planned). Only experienced testers were encouraged to participate.

On the 24th August 2017, Bittrex announced their full support for the transition of V2 DMD to V3 DMD. Users on the exchange who kept their DMD units of account on Bittrex would see all their balance totals reflect what they had prior to the 1:1 swap. Trading there would recommence once they received confirmation from the DMD Foundation that the transition had been successful. They finished by saying:

"Note: Bittrex will be closing our DMD wallet and stop trading the token to take accurate snapshots of balances. If any DMD deposits you had sent to Bittrex are not settled (e.g. marked as pending) by 6:00 pm PT on 9/11/2017 (1:00 am UTC on 9/12/2017), you may not be credited with DMD."

From the beginning to the end of August, the market capitalisation of Diamond had more or less doubled. Figures from www.coinmarketcap.com are:

Date	Low US$	Open US$	Close US$	High US$	Volume US$	Market Cap US$
1st August	2.75	2.95	3.13	3.54	122,391	6,517,760
31st August	5.59	5.70	6.20	6.40	217,479	12,857,100

On the 29th August at 21:43:47 UTC, user "popshot" published a simple guide on how to prepare for the upcoming blockchain transition. He wanted everyone to be as confident as possible. Three methods were available:

- Export private keys of your DMD Diamond Wallet 2.0 address and import it to the new DMD Diamond Wallet 3.0

- Move your copy of wallet.dat file (which holds all your private keys) from DMD Diamond 2.0 folder into DMD Diamond 3.0 wallet folder.

- If you hold coins in an exchange wait till they update to the new blockchain.

As had been well known for some time, direct DMD proof of work mining was coming to an end. Both major DMD mining pools (danbi's and Miningfield) were set to close on the 12th September 2017. Pool mining at danbi's ceased on the 1st September 2017. Both the DMD Multipool and Cloudmining services would still continue after the transition, but multipool pay outs would be halted between the 10th and 14th September.

On the 13th September, the last block timestamped to the V2 blockchain. A snapshot of this blockchain happened at block number 2,366,375 after which any mining, transactions and staking would not be recognised until the V3 blockchain became live. A total of 2,278,447.86053872 DMD were generated by the old chain:

Block #2,366,375 (Reward 0.077397 DMD) September 13th 2017 at 12:15:32 PM UTC

First block of the new V3 blockchain timestamped:

Block #1 (Reward 2,428,500 DMD) September 14th 2017 at 07:20:32 PM UTC

For the first week, network block rewards were 99% less at 0.0235 DMD in order to give everyone ample time to set up their PoS wallet clients and masternodes. Some time after block number 1,400 on the 15th September, once PoS had been made mature via PoW, the developers released version 3.0.0.12 of the wallet clients.

The DMD Foundation, and the community as a whole, were happy about the successful transition. It had laid the foundations for further expansion of the DMD network. Many improvements were planned going forward into 2018 in terms of security, speed and privacy. Also, the value of one unit of DMD account was surging towards US$12. A quote from the DMD Foundation was:

"We are excited about the future and feel that DMD Diamond is on the path to become a strong and recognizable monetary system on the cryptocurrency market that empowers people to achieve financial freedom. The advent of Diamond Master Nodes will inevitably further increase the value of DMD and form the foundations for future services linked to DMD Diamond ecosystem."

APPENDIX

Diamond 2.0—The Phoenix of Cryptocurrency

Article written by Razvan "Spiry"

July 17, 2014

Well it's been a long time since we've done a coin review, due the fact that most of cryptocurrencies now hold up at most a few months then they are gone after developers had a major dump on its investors—99% of cases are like that. However this one, is different, because Diamond celebrates its 1st year in existence on the market.

Diamond has been through ups & downs from the beginning with just a simple launch and not much word from the developer or a bigger plan expert, its scarity making it very hard to attack and creating a slow mining pace assuring it a long lasting future. It is one of the first cryptocurrecnies that got on market after Bitcoin with no premine & fair public launch, featuring Proof-of-Stake, Random Blocks and Transaction Messages.

The name "Diamond" is perfect for what it needs to express, since it's very rare with only 4.38 million coins to be issued. Also a slow paced mining and minting process, makes it very hard to acquire large amounts of Dimaonds, exactly like in real life. Also its trade symbol is "DMD".

Scrypt to Groestl Algorithm Transition, Change of Development Team & More

Diamond started with a developer who didn't do much except launching the coin that was fair and with NO Pre-mine or IPO involved. Everything was good and working for some good months without any intervention from developer, but once it appeared to be abandoned by its developer, the community started to maintain it.

They already had plans to move from Scrypt to Groestl algorithm as a form of prevention from Scrypt ASICs to attack on the network or abuse it, but the abuse had aleady started with the infamous bug "Time Warp Attack". The community had to rollout the plan of algorithm change even faster than actually announced so they could fix the bug and keep Diamond alive and boosting it up to a new era of evolution with a new and more efficient algorithm "Groestl". Being a very hard transition Diamond now have a part of its blockchain hashed under Scrypt Algorithm and the second new part started on Groestl Algorithm.

Now it is time for a serious Development Team to kick-in with plans for Android Wallet, Multipool with Diamond Payouts, UI Redesign, Merge Mining and also other plans that we can't disclose them at the moment since, Diamond Development Team don't like to create hype without any results at hand. They are having plans and wish to create a stability and a future for Diamond. They wanted Diamond to address to peoples needs and their vision of a secure, fast % easy-to-use cryptocurrency.

Their newest Diamond wallet release confirmed the commitment to Diamond development. With this update they have introduced Fast Index feature speeding up client loading time significantly, Coin Control for wiser management of Diamonds, info tooltips and several other core code optimisations.

Diamond community have been through a lot, but now they've prevailed and they are still here, considering 0% premine & fair launch. It's a great achievement considering that a lot of coins have failed even with IPO and Investors lot of coin's have failed. Diamond will remain one of our favourite cryptocurrencies on the market because of its activity, constant evolution with community effort, only 500,000 Diamonds issued so far and also because it has 30+ years rollout plan which gives it status of Medium-Long Term Investment. In my opinion it's a cryptocurrency that worth to be bought bit by bit. But that's my personal view. Trade at your own risk.

GIVEAWAY: Thanks for staying with us and reading our article. If you leave is a feedback via comment form below with your Diamond Wallet address you will receive FEE DMD!

Our DMD address for contributions:
dccpDqUE8TSCVDkF7LnVxXmC1XDBEqHWMh

2 Years in Development Valuable Bitcoin Alternative Diamond Coin (DMD) Offers 50% Annual Interest

Bitcoin Press Release: Backed by the Diamond Foundation and an array of price stability mechanisms and professional services, long term valuable digital currency DMD is a stand-out in an increasingly crowded digital currency space. DMD is soon to celebrate its second birthday.

With almost 2 years of ongoing development, Diamond Coin's philosophy is to create long term stability through sensible management and an ever expanding network of supporting services. Diamond Coin strives to be a stable and secure digital currency with 50% interest annually and advanced security protocols and algorithms.

The team's unique approach overcomes challenges like inflation control, price volatility, security and sustainability by incentivizing holding rather than spending. Diamond Coin's future plans involve an entire ecosystem of Bitcoin 2.0 decentralized services with an increasing spectrum of digital currency financial instruments.

DMD stake holders are automatically eligible for 50% interest per annum in a straightforward process known as "minting". When minting the DMD adopter obtains some coins, and holds them in the Diamond Wallet for a given period of time which in turn generates new coins. Minting withdraws the DMD from the supply chain for staking, contributing to price stability, as well as securing the network through improved Proof-of-Stake technology.

In order to control DMD inflation and bring it in line with the annual rate of physical gold extraction, minting rewards will be successively reduced over the coming decades. The early adoption period for Diamond Coin has been set to last for a few years; a time frame that is uncommon in the digital currency industry. This requires a long term commitment that will translate into a slow but cumulative effect of organic growth. Such a model is also a pledge on behalf of the DMD developers to think strategically and long term.

To deal with price volatility the Diamond Coin ecosystem currently has two key mechanisms to help ensure the value remains stable. The first is the Diamond Multipool that allows participants with their own computer hardware to mine currencies with almost any algorithm and receive DMD in return. The second service Diamond Cloud Mining enables anyone to collectively mine BTC in the cloud and convert this into DMD payouts. The system has proven to be adaptive, sustainable and rewarding for its participants.

The Diamond Coin Foundation developers treat network security as a continuous challenge that needs to be addressed and developed to remain a step ahead of potential security threats. Improvements in protocols and software optimizations provide a streamlined client for the end user. Employing a Hybrid Security of two separate protocols working in tandem is the cornerstone of Diamond Coin's security. To further strengthen security Diamond Coin implements 'Reactor', a protection tool that provides the benefit of additional safeguards along with the price stability mechanism of Diamond Cloud Mining.

Visit the official DMD website for more information:
https://bit.diamonds/

To trade DMD with Bitcoin please go to:
https://www.cryptsy.com/markets/view/DMD_BTC

Trade DMD on Bittrex:
https://bittrex.com/Market/Index?MarketName=BTC-DMD

Visit Diamond Coin on bitcointalk:
https://bitcointalk.org/index.php?topic=580725

Follow DMD on twitter: http://twitter.com/dmdcoin

How Anyone Can Make Money With Digital Currency: Bitcoin Alternative DMD Explains

7th September 2015

This is a <u>*Bitcoin Press Release*</u>*: Backed by the Diamond Foundation and an array of price stability mechanisms and professional services,* <u>*long term valuable digital currency DMD's team*</u>*believes in the potential of cryptocurrency for wealth creation worldwide. DMD recently celebrated its second birthday.*

The digital currency industry – while met with controversy in both the governmental and financial sector – has grown rapidly since Bitcoin was first created by Satoshi Nakamoto. Unlike fiat money cryptocurrency is not produced by banks and controlled by governments. It is cheap to transfer and can be protected against inflation. Cryptocurrencies may invoke a paradigm shift to the people's advantage, especially in countries with restricted finances, as well as to aid the millions of unbanked worldwide.

Cryptocurrencies have two ways of controlling how many coins should exist; 'Proof-of-Work', and Proof-of-Stake', also known as 'minting'. Mining is the process of adding transaction records to the public ledger through computers solving algorithms. This is the method used when producing Bitcoins. Mining requires a steep learning curve and an initial investment that ranges from a few dollars in a mining pool to several thousand dollars for a physical miner. Mining also requires continuous reinvestment in computer hardware and electricity; which for many poses a significant entry barrier. Proof-of-Stake, on the other hand, is a virtualization of the above process which achieves the same result but is more cost- and energy efficient and requires less expertise from the individual. <u>DMD Diamond combines the strengths of both</u> to create a hybrid system that is not only very effective at securing the network but also highly rewarding for DMD users.

Minting through Proof-of-Stake delivers interest like a bank, however due to the fact that it is not establishment centric, but user oriented, the amount of interest the individual receives is incomparably higher. DMD Diamond's network algorithms guarantee DMD adopter's 50% interest annually which in real terms means that a deposited 1000 DMD will yield an additional 500 DMD hands-free. To use a DMD Diamond wallet is as simple as opening the wallet and keeping it running in the background on a PC. This makes DMD an optimal choice for novice and tech-savvy users alike. Diamond's system is programmed to function automatically and maximize profits for DMD adopters, and not to make profit from users as in traditional banking.

In order to increase the DMD adopters wealth with 50% annually without causing hyperinflation and loss of value Diamond's system is governed by a predefined and carefully designed issuance model. The model takes into account all possible outcomes and any increase of coin count – created by any number of participants – so that a collapse of DMD Diamond monetary system is at all time prevented. DMD Diamond takes a constantly decreasing inflation approach with the ultimate aim of achieving inflation at par with yearly world gold excavation.

In a time where the banking sector has proven to be unstable and world governments constantly change interest rates, DMD Diamond brings stability with predefined cryptographic algorithms. Modern businesses in any country, with any regime are able to plan not only months but decades ahead when implementing DMD Diamond to their business.

Visit the official DMD website for more information:
https://bit.diamonds/

To trade DMD with Bitcoin please go to:
https://www.cryptsy.com/markets/view/DMD_BTC

Trade DMD on Bittrex:
https://bittrex.com/Market/Index?MarketName=BTC-DMD

Visit Diamond Coin on bitcointalk:
https://bitcointalk.org/index.php?topic=580725

Follow DMD on twitter:
http://twitter.com/dmdcoin

www.ingramcontent.com/pod-product-compliance
Lightning Source LLC
Chambersburg PA
CBHW071008050326
40689CB00014B/3534